The American Battle Monu

G000150672

WHEN THE AKIMOTOS WENT TO WAR

An untold story of family, patriotism, and sacrifice
during World War II

Matthew Elms

Printed in the United States of America

For information to reproduce selections from the book, write to

American Battle Monuments Commission

2300 Clarendon Blvd, Suite 500

Arlington, VA 22201

www.abmc.gov

ISBN 978-0-9790266-4-5

AMERICAN BATTLE
MONUMENTS COMMISSION

"Time will not dim the glory of their deeds."
GENERAL OF THE ARMIES JOHN J. PERSHING

TABLE OF CONTENTS

MAPS

Foreward

I am proud to be Secretary of one of the U.S. government's most honorable agencies, the American Battle Monuments Commission (ABMC). While we are a small agency in terms of resources, we are large in scope and mission. We have the responsibility to maintain and care for 25 cemeteries and 27 monuments, memorials and markers across the globe. Within those cemeteries we honor more than 200,000 Americans that gave their lives in World War I and World War II.

But as generations pass, we become further removed from these two conflicts that shaped the twentieth century and our world today, creating the possible reality that future generations of Americans will not understand the sacrifices born by our country in the defense of freedom. We have no living World War I veterans, and our World War II veterans won't be with us for much longer. Their voices, stories and memories will fade unless we work to reverse this course.

When I reflect on this reality, the words of the early twentieth century poet, Archibald MacLeish, who lost his brother Kenneth in World War I, come to mind. MacLeish wrote in his poem, "The Young Dead Soldiers Do Not Speak," "Our deaths are not ours: they are yours, they will mean what you make them.....We leave you our deaths. Give them their meaning. We were young, they say. We have died; remember us."

It's clear that we at the ABMC must bring his words to life. We have to carry forward their stories and their legacies ensuring Americans learn about those who gave "the last full measure of devotion," as Abraham Lincoln phrased it in the Gettysburg Address.

Each American honored in an ABMC cemetery has a story. Every person represents a father, mother, sister, brother, husband, wife, or child. Every one of these individuals contributed to the freedoms and liberties we hold dear today. This is why ABMC embarked on this *Understanding Sacrifice* project with National History Day and the Roy Roszenweig Center for History and New Media at George Mason University. We want our nation's young people to hear those voices so that they can carry forward MacLeish's call.

And this book, written by a teacher participating in the *Understanding Sacrifice* program, brings to fruition MacLeish's words. The Akimoto brothers were not regular Americans – they were Nisei – first generation born Japanese Americans. At the outset of World War II, Japanese Americans across the country faced hatred and discrimination. Their financial assets and accounts were frozen. Their business were closed. They were evicted from their homes and relocated to internment camps out of fear that they were spies or saboteurs. The U.S. government did this without due process because of simple bigotry and fear.

Despite this, these three brothers still enlisted in the U.S. Army. They did so because they believed in something higher than themselves. Even with the shame of relocation and the insult of being stripped of basic civil rights, they chose to serve their country. It is easy to look back on history and condemn the U.S. government for its actions during the war, but that has already been done. It is much more difficult to look forward into the future and ensure Americans, such as the Akimoto brothers are forever remembered for their selfless actions and sacrifice that allowed liberty to triumph over tyranny. That is what MacLeish challenges us to do – to be the voices of the men and women who no longer speak.

Matthew Elms, the author of this incredible story, gives the Akimoto brothers that voice that will now be heard in classrooms and living rooms around the world. He has created a book that gives meaning to the deaths of Johnny and Victor Akimoto, and my hope is that you'll give meaning to these brothers as you share and discuss their story with your friends, family and classmates. More than 405,300 Americans died in World War II. Give their deaths meaning!

Most Respectfully,

Max Cleland
Secretary, American Battle Monuments Commission

Acknowledgments

Between these pages is the story of the Akimoto brothers, uncovered and retold through the foresight of the American Battle Monuments Commission (ABMC). Specifically, ABMC Secretary Max Cleland and Chief of External Affairs Tim Nosal have found a way to give back to America. Through the dedicated efforts of 18 teachers in the *Understanding Sacrifice* program, students from around the world will learn about the vital contributions of Americans during World War II.

Dr. Cathy Gorn and Lynne O'Hara at National History Day (NHD) have worked tirelessly to bring this story into print. NHD endeavors to engage middle and high school students in historical research projects in order to bring our youth to a more complex understanding of the world around them. Along with them, Jennifer Rosenfeld at the Roy Rosenzweig Center for History and New Media and Dr. Christopher Hamner at George Mason University have given their guidance throughout.

Singapore American School (SAS) is an extraordinary school. Financial support and encouragement from administrators Dr. Chip Kimball, Dr. Jennifer Sparrow, and Devin Pratt, made this book possible. Thank you to my colleagues Rebecca Clark, Betsy Hall, Melissa Trainor, Dan Chassagne, Jim Ryan, Scott Oskins, Dr. Vicki Rogers, Julie Goode, and Brian Arleth for suffering through early versions. Within this group of colleagues I must mention the amazing Scott Riley who pointed the way to this lost pilot. Visiting authors Susan Campbell Bartolleti, Eric Rohman, and Candice Fleming gave me the encouragement to persevere.

At the heart of any good school lie the students, our hope for tomorrow. I want to thank Ruth Jaensubhakij, Hana Matsudaira,

Andrew Rhee, Sam Sequiera Iyer, Cristina Escajadillo, Thani Greco, Charles LaNasa, Anna Bierley, Alex Danielson, and Claire Schwarze, for reading critically and making suggestions to their half-crazed teacher. I need to make special mention of Priyanka Aiyer and my friend in baseball, Kianna Broadman, for their critiques, support, and laughter over the years.

I also want to thank my team of German translators, including Mary Johnson, Stephanie Zarikow, Thomas Schulz, and Peter Schellenberger—your efforts have made a remarkable difference in understanding the complete story.

A number of individuals and organizations provided services and information. These include Tom Ikeda and Caitlyn Oiye at Densho, Barbara Watanabe at the Go For Broke Educational Foundation, Charlyn Dote at the 100th Infantry Battalion Veterans Education Center, and Michael Yaguchi at the Pan Pacific American Leaders and Mentors organization. A special thank you to Peter Koby for his help designing the maps to help make the book more accessible to readers.

Clearly, this story would not exist without the Akimoto family. To all of them, great-grandparents down to the most recent additions, thank you for your time, effort, and patriotism. As much as I am thankful for the military service of Victor, Johnny, and Ted, I truly appreciate the kindness and warmth of the entire Akimoto family.

Finally, thank you to my parents, Tom and Clare, for their reassurance, enthusiasm, and special mailing abilities. Alicia, Cameron, and Callie, thanks for letting your father have a frenetic year to fulfill a lifetime dream. And to my wife, Dr. Deborah Elms, thank you for seeing the possibilities within me.

Dedication

To the memory of Mary Miki Shiratori Akimoto, who understood the meaning of sacrifice (1889 – 1979).

CHAPTER ONE

Battlefields of France, October 1944

The slightest movement of his right leg sent searing pain up Victor Akimoto's spine. He clutched the injury and waited for the arrival of medics in the tiny village of Biffontaine, France. Unable to move, his thigh bone shattered by a German bullet, he lay on the ground, consoling the injured soldiers around him. One man had been wounded by a large piece of shrapnel, a sharp metal fragment of a bomb that had pierced his back and protruded through his stomach. One of Victor's officers, Korean-American Second Lieutenant Young-Oak "Samurai" Kim, had a severe injury to his right hand and was losing consciousness due to blood loss.

Victor Akimoto, c. 1943 (Akimoto Family Collection)

Japanese-American infantrymen of the 100th Infantry Battalion, 442nd Regimental Combat Team in France, 1944 *(The U.S. Army Center of Military History)*

In the heavily wooded northern French Vosges Mountains, the struggle to rescue the Lost Battalion of World War II raged outside the doorway. Nearby, the German army surrounded the soldiers of the 141st Infantry Regiment from Texas who huddled in emergency foxholes to escape the assault. German artillery pounded their location from all sides. Bomb bursts and machine gun fire sent out chattering waves of deadly metal.

Victor's unit, A Company, 100th Infantry Battalion, had deployed to provide an escape route for the 141st Infantry. His company cleared most of the French hamlet of Biffontaine. While they were securing the last parts of the village, several German infantrymen refused to give ground. His unit then fell back to a more secure location.

Allied Military Advance, October 1944

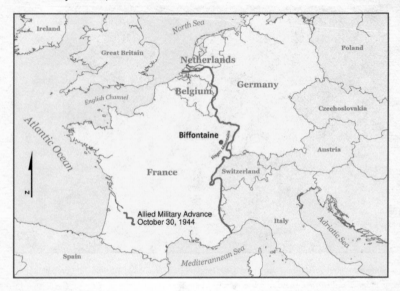

By late October 1944, Allied military forces had advanced through northern France and were positioned on the German border (Peter Koby).

Knowing his platoon needed to retreat, Victor sheltered behind a large tree. Ammunition loaded, gun raised, Victor provided covering fire until his unit reached safety behind several stone buildings. He turned to run as machine gun fire erupted. A bullet caught his right leg and he collapsed. He crawled into a foxhole and called out, "Medic, Medic!"

Private Stanley Izumigawa dove into Victor's foxhole. As he prepared to bandage Victor's leg, a mortar shell exploded with a flash. Dirt covered both men. More help soon arrived, and rushed Victor to a nearby farmhouse.

Later that evening with hands aloft and guns at their backs, several captured Germans soldiers arrived at the farmhouse. Other members of Victor's A Company, 100th Infantry Battalion had managed to push the Germans back and take the prisoners.

Victor lay on his back, with his leg tightly bandaged, while the rest of A Company battled through the town. Medical help arrived at the makeshift aid station just after sunset. Sergeant Jimmie Kanaya, one of the battalion's medics, got to work assessing each man. He provided clean bandages, sulfa powder and pills to prevent infections, and morphine injections to reduce pain.

Due to the steep mountain terrain Victor's unit remained out of radio contact with the rear area, nearly two miles away. With night falling fast, the men knew help would not arrive soon. The medical staff wanted to evacuate the injured soldiers as soon as possible. With time running out and night turning to morning, the officers had to make a decision. They would wait until just before dawn to load the wounded onto stretchers. By sunrise, however, they did not have enough men to carry the injured through the rugged hills and also guard the POWs.

Despite his injuries Second Lieutenant Kim, helped to formulate a plan. The head of the column would carry a white hospital flag with a red cross, to prevent attacks, while the POWs would carry the

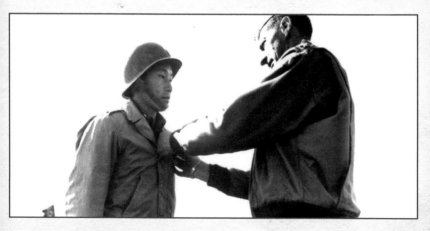

Young Oak Kim receives an award, c. 1944 *(University of Southern California Libraries)*

stretchers. The other Americans would guard the POWs. Organizing a single-file stretcher train, they set off.

Confusion soon reigned. They reversed course due to smashed trails, scorched earth, and shattered timbers. They became lost and disoriented. Poor maps and destroyed physical markers made navigation all but impossible. Bombs burst and battles raged as the 141st Infantry Regiment, known as the Lost Battalion, clung to survival nearby. The smell of acrid gunpowder, burning wood, and nervous fear filled the air with dread. A bewildered French farmer gave them wrong directions. They turned again. Large explosions rocked the earth. The POWs were by then struggling to carry the injured.

All at once, the column clattered to a stop.

CHAPTER TWO

THE AKIMOTO FAMILY

Victor's father, Masanori Akimoto, entered the United States on August 26, 1897. Born in Aomori-Inagaki in the northern part of Honshu, Japan in 1886, he came from a family that owned land in that prestigious town, noted for the summer palace of the imperial family.

Japan, Pre-World War II

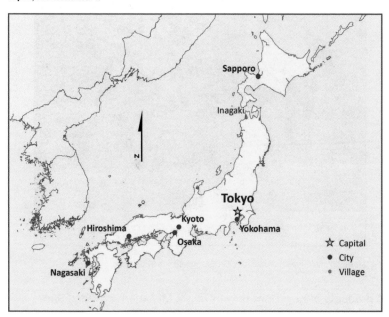

Japan before Worl War II (Peter Koby)

1906
L TO R: HIDE SHIRATORI, DAD, RENKICHI AKIMOTO

Masanori (middle) with brothers, c. 1906 (Akimoto Family Collection)

A graduate of Keio University in Tokyo, Masanori arrived in San Francisco in the late summer in 1897, intending to enroll at Princeton University. Wearing a fancy tailored suit and a bowler hat, he traveled by train across the country. Curious about Native

American tribes near Salt Lake City, Utah, he impulsively jumped off the train. There, Masanori met some Mormon businessmen who showed him the town and the nearby Native American reservation. The businessmen offered him a job on the spot. For nearly eight years he ran their agricultural operations.

Masanori returned to Japan to visit his family, proud to show off his savings and eager to find a bride. But his parents were not pleased to discover Masanori had never reached Princeton. He quickly became the shame of the family.

The woman who would eventually become Victor's mother, Mary "Miki" Shiratori, was born in August 1888 to a prominent samurai family. A true beauty, she had a bright future in Japan. Miki must have been persuasive in her early years. She convinced her father to allow her to attend an Episcopal missionary school. Devoting herself to teaching, she began instructing pupils at the age of 18. Eventually she converted to Christianity and added "Mary" to her name.

Mary "Miki" Shiratori, Japan, 1906 (Akimoto Family Collection)

15

When Masanori told his father confidentially, "I'm going to marry that woman," his father reminded him that he had brought shame upon the whole family and would never be permitted to marry someone of Mary's status. Yet Masanori had a trick up his sleeve. He convinced Mary's parents that ruthless gangsters would soon kidnap her, a rumor he had started. Thus, Masanori appeared as an eligible suitor for Mary, seemingly saving the day. They married on May 25, 1906. After the birth of their first child, Masanori brought his wife and child back to the United States.

Mary "Miki" Shiratori with her first pupils, c. 1907 (Akimoto Family Collection)

As an *Issei*, Masanori was not permitted to become a U.S. citizen due to anti-Asian immigration laws. Despite his non-citizen status, in 1918 he registered for the World War I draft. Fortunately for Masanori, the war ended before he was called up. Instead, on the windswept, fertile farmlands of Idaho, Masanori and Mary began raising a large family with four girls—Ruth, Margaret, Martha, and Jane—and four boys—Ned, Victor, Ted, and Johnny.

A ninth child was born between Johnny and Jane. Family friends down the street from the Akimotos could not have children, so Masanori and Mary gave them Fred, a son to carry on their family name. But when he was two years old, Fred died of pneumonia.

Child Giving

The custom of giving a child away to a family without children is still practiced in some societies. In some traditional Polynesian cultures, such as Hawaii, the well-documented tradition of giving away a child is referred to as "hanai" or "ho'okama."

Masanori rarely showed anger as he and Mary raised their large brood of children. When he did, the kids listened. He once overheard Victor's younger brother Ted complain about a friend who promised to pay him back the loan of a quarter but was a week late in repaying his debt. Masanori shouted at Ted, "I never want to hear you complaining or arguing about food or money! That is vulgar! You never loan money to a friend, you give it to him. This way he won't feel guilty that he can't pay you back and you won't feel resentful because he hasn't paid you. But you must convince him that you are giving it to him as a sacrifice that you are willing to make. If he is the friend you think he is, he will give it back to you when he can."

Ted and Johnny Akimoto, Idaho, 1925
(Akimoto Family Collection)

18

When Victor was six, an event occurred that changed the course of his life. As he was going to bed one evening in Idaho, a group of boys scared and taunted him outside his window. He soon began to lose large clumps of hair. The shock of being scared so badly caused his hair follicales to stop producing hair. Local doctors hoped that Victor's hair would recover from the shock. The family decided to move to Los Angeles for better health care. Mary and Masanori hoped the doctors in Los Angeles could help him, but they could not. Victor was diagnosed as suffering from a severe case of alopecia, or sudden hair loss. Throughout his life, Victor Akimoto was just plain bald. To hide his shiny dome in photographs, he nearly always wore a hat. The move to Los Angeles would later prove to have a profound effect on the fate of the Akimoto family.

Alopecia

A medical condition thought to be caused by an autoimmune reaction. Triggered by viruses, medicines, infections, or other environmental causes, the immune system sends out white blood cells to attack foreign bodies. In Victor's case, the white blood cells attacked his hair follicles, making them incapable of producing hair.

In Los Angeles, Mary raised the eight children while Masanori went to work selling life insurance. During the Great Depression of the 1930s, Victor and the other children overheard their parents having a loud argument. Mary became upset upon learning that Masanori had given a 100-pound bag of rice to a widow with children. The life insurance policy he had sold the family before the father's sudden death became worthless when the insurance company went out of business. Regardless, Masanori continued to make sacrifices to help the widow. He gave the single mother food and money to compensate for their lost insurance. Mary, thinking of their struggles to feed their own children, berated Masanori. Finally, Masanori turned to his wife and asserted, "Don't you realize that you at least have me to help? I will hear no more about it."

Principles such as giving to others, honoring your family, and loyalty to country were part of Victor's upbringing. The Akimotos respected living an honorable life as a person of character. True gifts, the children learned, were given willingly, without the expectation of repayment. When Masanori died years later, all of the young Akimotos understood the pile of envelopes that came in with notes saying, "I would like to give back what Masanori gave me."

Victor Akimoto in his early 20s with his nephew, Jon Kodani, c. 1940 (Akimoto Family Collection)

Victor demonstrated leadership while growing up. He would show the other children in the Los Angeles neighborhood how to build rubber band guns, how to make slingshots from discarded lumber, and how to construct matchstick guns from a clothespin.

If one of his siblings found a discarded roller skate, Victor knew what to do. Deciding scooters were too babyish, he instead built a shallow board slightly larger than his foot, removed the clamps from the skate, and nailed it to the bottom of the board. Next, he hammered a piece of wood across the toe to hold the skate onto the wooden board. Soon kids like Johnny and Ted rode some of the first skateboards in Los Angeles.

Johnny Akimoto, c. 1930 (Akimoto Family Collection)

At times, Victor's role as a neighborhood leader made life difficult for some of the younger Akimotos. As one of the older brothers and a firm believer in tough love and fair play, he made it plain to his younger siblings, Ted and Johnny, that he would not show them any favoritism on the streets.

Victor attended the 36th Street Elementary School, Forshay Junior High School, and Jacob Riis High School in Los Angeles, California, where he was a talented, all-around star athlete.

Ted Akimoto, c. 1940 (Akimoto Family Collection)

Ted, with his wavy and curly hair, did not want to follow in the accomplished shadow of his older brother. He attended Poly High School in Los Angeles, played on the football team, and took photos as a member of the photography club. Johnny developed into an excellent athlete as well. He had remarkable upper-body strength, which he developed through gymnastics and weight-lifting. Johnny developed the build of a soldier from an early age.

As he grew, Victor held a variety of jobs, including working at a fruit stand, selling goods with a wholesaler, and driving a delivery truck throughout Los Angeles.

On December 7, 1941, everything changed.

Johnny Akimoto on the rings, c. 1941 (Akimoto Family Collection)

22

CHAPTER THREE

Captives in France, October 1944

Amid the roar of artillery shells and distant mortar explosions, the stretcher train rattled to a halt in the Vosges Forest in France. As the stretcher bearers hesitated, fear gripped Victor's heart. Each man knew only one reason for the column to come to such an abrupt halt. In the midst of the battles surrounding them, the soldiers heard shouts from the red cross flag bearer at the front, calling for the officers in charge. As the officers made their way forward, each man contemplated his options; try to escape and risk being shot, or become captured and risk death as a prisoner of war at the hands of the Germans.

Second Lieutenant Kim knew he had to escape. Without antibiotics and proper medical treatment for his injured hand, he would suffer a long and painful death in a German prisoner of war (POW) camp.

"Samurai" Kim also knew that if captured, he could be a danger to U.S. troops. As his unit's intelligence officer, he risked revealing secrets to the Germans while under interrogation. Kim quietly rolled off his stretcher and Medic Richard Chenin, noticing his struggles to move, gathered Kim under his shoulder. Leaving Victor and the other injured behind, they slipped into some nearby bushes to hide from the enemy. Kim winced helplessly as he watched the German POWs become the guards for the captured Americans. Eventually,

Kim and Chenin would make it back to the American lines where Kim reported what had happened to the rest of the men.

Meanwhile, the intervening German Army reversed the course of war for the captured Americans. Flying the red cross flag with guns deployed was against the rules of war. This violation of the Geneva Conventions infuriated the Germans. Victor, injured too badly to resist or escape, prayed for a reprieve from the Germans. His prayers went unanswered.

Geneva Conventions

The Geneva Conventions are a series of treaties concerning the treatment of civilians, prisoners of war (POWs), and soldiers who are otherwise incapable of fighting.

Jimmie Kanaya, one of the medics who had remained with the prisoners, continued to tend to the GIs as best as he could without proper supplies.

Second Lieutenant Jimmie Kanaya, c. 1943 (Courtesy of Jimmie Kanaya)

The stretcher train set off in the opposite direction, toward the German lines, through the battle scarred woods. Up rocky hills, across streams cluttered with shattered trees, through smoke-filled ravines, Victor Akimoto and the other wounded suffered through the punishing march into enemy territory.

At one point an American patrol nearly discovered the column, but the Germans forced the GIs to keep quiet. Then the stretcher train resumed its travels. Through the murkiness caused by morphine injections, Victor slowly began to come to terms with his situation. Right leg injured, unable to escape, a prisoner of the Germans, his chances of survival hung in the balance.

CHAPTER FOUR

PEARL HARBOR, DECEMBER 7, 1941

On December 7, 1941, Japan bombed Pearl Harbor, on the island of Oahu, Hawaii, and propelled the United States into World War II. Within hours of the attack, anti-Japanese hysteria swept across America, especially in California, Oregon, and Washington.

Pearl Harbor, December 7, 1941 (Courtesy of the *Franklin D. Roosevelt Presidential Library and Museum*)

The next day, enraged by the attacks by Japan, Victor enlisted in the U.S. Army with thousands of other Americans. Enormously proud of their son, the Akimoto family gathered to celebrate Victor's pending military service to his country. Victor initially became a role model for his brothers. His example also motivated other Nisei men and women who would eventually volunteer for military service during World War II.

Back row left to right: Martha, John, Ned, and Hideo. Front row: Mary, Victor, Masanori, and Ruth. The small child is Jon Kodani. This photograph was most likely taken by Ted after Victor's enlistment, January 1942. (Akimoto Family Collection)

Victor Akimoto, c. 1942 (Akimoto Family Collection)

Victor never expressed any concern about his Japanese ancestry or a trepidation about fighting against the Japanese. He simply wanted to defend his country, the United States of America.

Unfortunately, on January 7, 1942, the Federal Bureau of Investigation arrested Victor for gambling, a minor crime. Yet his arrest became an embarrassment to his family at a time when Japanese

Americans faced increased scrutiny. Inducted into the service on January 27, 1942, he was sent to the frigid cold of Fort Warren, Wyoming. In his first letter home, he wrote,

February 8, 1942

Dear members of the Akimoto clan,

This is just a line from the ebony colored sheep of the family reporting that he has reached his destination in good shape and is starting out to do his bit for Uncle Sam....Since I came here alone they put me in a barrack with a bunch of fellows from Minnesota and Missouri but I get along all right as there [sic] swell fellows.

Vic

Letter from Victor Akimoto to his family, February 8, 1942. (Akimoto Family Collection)

Uncle Sam (initials U.S.) is a common personification of the United States government. J.M. Flagg's 1917 World War I poster is one of the most popular illustrations of Uncle Sam. (*Library of Congress*)

The United States during World War II

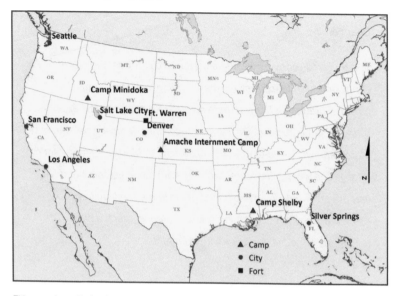

This map shows the key locations where the Akimoto family traveled during World War II.
(Peter Koby)

Victor met people from across America while driving military trucks, learning how to care for weapons, and attending a variety of classes about subjects such as the Articles of War. Like most soldiers, however, he worried about the plight of his family back home. A few weeks later, he wrote,

Articles of War

Codes and rules of conduct that all U.S. military personnel follow. This includes penalties for desertion, treason, and criminal activity.

February 18, 1942

Dear Family,

Just received your very welcome carton of cigarettes and box of candy and wish to express my thanks. I know all of you must be having it pretty tough down there so please don't go to any expense by sending me packages as I will be receiving my pay on the first of March and will be quite wealthy...According to Martha's letter [older sister] I see where Ned [older brother] wants to enlist too, but if his feet are still weak I'd advise him to enlist in the Medical Corps or some branch where you don't have to march so much as this drilling would be hell for a guy with bum feet...

Letter from Victor Akimoto to his family, February 18, 1942 (Akimoto Family Collection)

Meanwhile, on Dayton Street in Los Angeles, California, the Akimotos opened their home to another Japanese-American family whose parents lost their jobs due to their Japanese ancestry. On February 19, 1942, President Franklin Delano Roosevelt issued Executive Order 9066, which changed the lives of hundreds of thousands of Japanese Americans living along the west coast of America. Within weeks, many Japanese Americans would be incarcerated. Even Theodor Geisel, better known as Dr. Seuss, portrayed Japanese Americans as traitors, wearing stereotypical bowler hats, round eyeglasses, and leering through slanted eyes. [1]

Dr. Seuss editorial cartoon, February 13, 1942. The "Honorable 5th Column" refers to an undercover Japanese spy organization. (*University of California, San Diego Library*)

In Wyoming, Victor was nursing an injured right hand. While on kitchen patrol, he had scalded the back of his hand with boiling water, resulting in a second-degree burn that took more than a month to heal.

April 29, 1942

Q.M. Detachment
Building 212

Dear Family,

Just received your letter today and sure am sorry for causing all of you to worry over me. Everything is fine out here so please don't worry as the only way I could ever suffer any serious casualty out here in these wild hills of Wyoming is by overeating. In fact the way things are shaping out there in Calif. it [is] the other way around and I'm worried about how you folks are going to get along.

As for my hand, it is just about healed now and by the end of this week I should be ready for duty again. It sure will feel good to start working again for it sure gets tiresome laying around the barracks as I've been doing for about a month now and the way I've been eating I think this month instead of the government paying me, I should pay them.

Vic.

P.S. You will have to excuse the writing as three of my fingers are still bandaged and its just awkward trying to write.

Letter from Victor Akimoto to his family, April 29, 1942. (Akimoto Family Collection)

Remarkably, even as his parents and siblings prepared to be forcibly removed from their home, Victor tried to find humor in the situation.

CHAPTER FIVE

TRAINING IN FORT WARREN, WYOMING, 1942

After his scalded hand healed, Victor spent much of his time mowing lawns and tending the gardens around Fort Warren.

Like millions of other American soldiers of World War II, he received immunizations, attended lectures, participated in physical training, and waited for his opportunity to defend America. Because of his Japanese ancestry, however, the U.S. Army declined to send Victor into battle.

He sent home money to his parents, took out life insurance, and managed to get furloughs home in September 1942 and

Victor Akimoto at Fort Warren, Wyoming, spring 1942 (Akimoto Family Collection)

December 1943. During this first visit, Victor most likely had a number of conversations with his mother and father concerning the potential enlistment of his younger brothers, Ted and Johnny. While his family witnessed rising racial tensions against Japanese

Americans, part of their hopes for the future rested on Victor's continuing service in the U.S. military. The Akimotos' hope: if Japanese Americans could serve bravely in the armed forces, then perhaps America would finally move beyond seeing people of Asian descent as a different people, a different race, and just see them as patriotic Americans.

This image from November 11, 1944 was seen on the door of a barber shop in Parker, Arizona, 15 miles from the Colorado River Relocation Center (also known as the Poston War Relocation Center.) Evacuees from the center, who could not leave its confines without a pass, were discouraged from shopping in Parker by War Relocation Authority officials. (*Densho* and the *National Archives Records Administration*)

Problems of race, marriage, and other family-related issues featured frequently in Victor's letters. In a rare and touching view into the relationship with his father, and his deeply held religious convictions, Victor wrote a carefully worded letter to his father concerning the upcoming marriage of his sister Martha to a Caucasian man, Peter Hamlet.

Technical Sergeant Victor Akimoto, early 1943 (Akimoto Family Collection)

34

November 21, 1942

Dear Dad,

...As for my opinion on the matters after thinking it over and over, I'm afraid I still find myself unfit and at a loss for an answer. For after all, only God up above can foresee whether their marriage will be one of happiness or not.

Still we all know how slim the chances for a happy marriage are when two such widely separated races marry on account of the invisible barriers of society that spring up in every day [sic] life as we have all found out through experience.

Thus, even though they love each other so deeply and believe that that is all that matters for a happy married life, they've got to realize that they cannot live in a world of their own but must live under the critical eyes of society....

So Dad, you talk to her, for according to the laws of society we all know which decision is right and which is wrong so if they still insist on marrying after reviewing the future they face, I can only say in closing that only God knows whether their decision is right or wrong.

Vic

P.S. I'm very sorry I will not be able to send you any money right away as I had a slight altercation with a couple of civilians and had to have some dentist work on my front teeth which set me back quite a bit. However as soon as that fat payday rolls around will send some pronto."

Letter from Victor Akimoto to his father, November 21, 1942 (Akimoto Family Collection)

The 1940s were an era of legalized segregation, Jim Crow laws, and overt racism. Public signs throughout the South designated where "Whites" and "Colored" could eat, drink, and swim. Additionally, racial "purity" laws throughout the United States declared interracial marriages illegal.

Reading between the lines in Victor's post-script reveals even more of the underlying racial tensions of the time. Victor had most certainly became involved in an "altercation" because of his ancestry.

While the loss of money from his private's pay may not seem like a big deal, it came as another blow to the struggling Akimoto family.

To prevent suspected Japanese sympathizers from sending money to Japan, the U.S. government froze the bank accounts and assets of those born in Japan, which meant that Masanori and Mary could not get access to their money. Now, in a reversal of generations, the parents had to rely on their children to support the family.

Victor Akimoto in his early 20s, c. 1942 (Akimoto Family Collection)

CHAPTER SIX

CAPTIVES IN AMERICA, 1942-1943

Watercolor of the Santa Anita Racetrack Assembly Center painted by Mary "Miki" Akimoto. Notice the guard towers with machine guns pointed toward the internment barracks. The small fort and post office fly the American flag outside the fence. The San Gabriel Mountains are portrayed in the background, c. 1942 (Akimoto Family Collection)

In February 1942, Executive Order 9066 sealed the fate of nearly 120,000 Japanese Americans. In the weeks and months that followed, Japanese Americans along the West Coast were forcibly rounded up and sent to assembly centers and later internment camps. While Victor trained with the U.S. Army to defend America, the U.S. Army put his own family under armed guard.

Japanese in Hawaii during World War II

Hawaii, a territory of the United States before and during World War II, interned a limited number of people of Japanese ancestry living on the islands. Under the protection of the United States, Lieutenant General Delos C. Emmons decided that internment was impractical for Hawaii because there were simply too many residents of Japanese origin. He defended the people of Japanese descent by citing the facts that no plots of espionage or spies within the Japanese community had been discovered since the bombing of Pearl Harbor.

Japanese-American evacuees under military armed guard at the Santa Anita Assembly Center, April 5, 1942 (*National Archives and Records Administration*)

Thousands of Japanese Americans sold their homes. Victor's family sold their home, as well as household furnishings and family heirlooms, at cut-rate prices. Items such as cameras, shortwave radios, and ceremonial Japanese swords were forbidden in the assembly and internment camps. These articles were discarded or sold, often for much less than their value.

The Akimoto family, which had called Dalton Avenue in Los Angeles their home for 16 years, filed their change of address card with the Department of Justice, Immigration and Naturalization Service and moved into Avenue G, Barrack 31, Unit 3 of the Santa Anita Horseracing Track: a horse stall. Family members made the best of it as they frantically searched for better options. Threatened with internment, Masanori and Mary, along with the younger kids, hoped to find jobs as laborers in the interior; they located jobs in Idaho with Masanori's former company, the Utah-Idaho Sugar Company. After moving to Idaho, however, they found themselves facing racial discrimination, slurs, and threats. They notified the Federal Bureau of Investigations (FBI) again and moved to Salt Lake City, Utah.

The Akimoto family and friends at a remodeled chicken coop in Idaho. Mary is second from the left in the front row. Ted is second from left in the second row. c. 1943 (Akimoto Family Collection)

Johnny, Victor's youngest brother, went ahead to the Amache Internment Camp near Granada, Colorado, during the winter of 1943. There, he avoided working for minimal wages as a farm laborer. He hoped to find better options. When Johnny arrived at the internment camp, he set about orienting himself to the layout and locating family friends. He quickly noticed the differences between this permanent internment camp and the temporary camp at Santa Anita, California.

39

February 3, 1943

Dear Mom & Dad,

Arrived in camp monday [sic] night. Everything is pretty good out here. Its [sic] not like Santa Anita though. I'm staying with Ioshi Mori & Yammy in a barracks. The floor is brick & the inside is like our bunkhouse, lined with seltex.[3] There's a coal stove in every barrack and they furnish all the coal. It sure is nice & warm in the room. I've seen Watada san already & he sends his regards. So far the food is pretty good. Haven't seen everybody yet cause the camp is pretty well spread out. Nothing more to write so I'll sign off. Say hi to Dot & Vic.

Just Johnny

Address: 6F – 3F
Amache Branch
Lamar, Colorado

Letter from Johnny Akimoto to his parents, February 3, 1943 (Akimoto Family Collection)

Life in Amache, like in all of the other nine internment camps, became a daily chore. The dusty and windy plains, far from the ski slopes of the Rocky Mountains, often forced internees indoors. Layers of dirt, dust, and grime covered everything indoors and out. The children went to school, and some adults

Internment

The word "internment" during World War II referred to the process and permanent encampments created by the U.S. government to isolate Japanese Americans. If you are interested in learning more about Japanese internment, visit: **www.densho.org**

Baseball game at the Amache Internment Camp, September 12, 1943 (*National Archives and Records Administration*)

found menial jobs within the camp or on nearby ranches. In the spring, baseball teams formed giving the internees a respite from their otherwise gloomy surroundings. The teams played under the watchful gaze of armed guards in elevated watchtowers. Outside the barracks, Japanese-style gardens popped up to give a bit of beauty to the otherwise drab and barren landscape.

Meanwhile, Victor's parents were still trying to stay out of the internment camps, working as laborers in Salt Lake City. By late 1942, with Mary in her mid-50s and Masanori in his 60s, the physical labor became increasingly difficult. They could not find sufficient work to support the family, and the racial harassment by locals became too much for them. By June 1943, Victor's parents had moved into Amache Internment Camp.

Mary "Miki" Shiratori Akimoto sits at a makeshift desk in her barracks at the Amache Internment Camp, c. 1944. (Akimoto Family Collection)

Civil Liberties Act of 1988

President Ronald Reagan signs the Civil Liberties Act of 1988 which granted repayment to those Japanese Americans interned by the United States government. (*Ronald Reagan Presidential Library*).

In 1988, President Ronald Reagan signed the Civil Liberties Act that publicly apologized for the incarceration of Japanese Americans and offered each survivor $20,000 in restitution. At the signing of the law, President Reagan stated, "Here we admit a wrong. Here we affirm our commitment as a nation to equal justice under the law."

CHAPTER SEVEN

THE AKIMOTO BROTHERS GO TO WAR 1943

Victor quickly moved through the enlisted ranks at Fort Warren. As he had enlisted at the age of 23, he was significantly older than the average World War II draftee. He started out as a private in January 1942, and his first promotion to private first class came in October of that same year. Yet even with positive reviews from his superiors, as an enlisted man of Japanese descent, his military career options were limited to menial labor and military police duty.

World War II U.S. Army Military Ranks	
Enlisted	
Private	Grade 7
Private First Class	Grade 6
Corporal	⎡ Grade 5
Technician Fifth Grade	⎣ Grade 5
Sergeant Technician Fourth Grade	⎡ Grade 4
Technician Fourth Grade	⎣ Grade 4
Staff Sergeant	⎡ Grade 3
Technician Third Grade	⎣ Grade 3
Technical Sergeant	Grade 2
First Sergeant	⎡ Grade 1
Master Sergeant	⎣ Grade 1
Officers	
Second Lieutenant	Lower Rank
First Lieutenant	
Captain	
Major	
Lieutenant Colonel	
Colonel	
Brigadier General	
Major General	
Lieutenant General	
General	Higher Rank

By the end of 1942, casualties were mounting in the Pacific and North African theaters of operations. Army recruitment officers needed thousands of infantry soldiers for the impending battles of Europe.

On January 31, 1943, President Roosevelt made a dramatic about-face, declaring, "The principle on which this country was founded and by which it has always been governed is that Americanism is a matter of heart and mind. Americanism is not, and never was, a matter of race or ancestry." He went on to say, "Every American should be given the opportunity to serve this country."

When Johnny heard about Roosevelt's announcement of the formation of an all-Japanese-American unit, he knew what he wanted to do. Eighteen days after arriving at Amache, Johnny sat down at a makeshift pinewood desk and wrote to his oldest sister and her husband about his plans.

Victor (left) and Johnny Akimoto (right) at Camp Shelby, Mississippi, 1943 (Akimoto Family Collection)

February 19, 1943

Dear Ruth & Hideo,

Well, I guess I might as well get to the point. I joined the army. I done a lot of thinking about it before I signed so don't think I done it on the spur of the moment.

You know I never did like any part of farming and about getting jobs in defense plants are a bunch of baloney. I didn't want to be a farm laborer, and don't want to stay in camp so I signed up.

Another thing, on our registration we got a couple of questions concerning our loyalty & willingness to fight for America. Well, to those two questions, 3 to 1 nusus[4] put no to that question. Well, that would take away all our rights & stuff. Well them dumb guys just make things tough for everybody else. Don't think I'm patriotic or stuff but I'm just looking out for myself. We'll be going the 1st of next month. Ask Ned if he wants my clothes or what. Only thing he probably could wear would be my shirts. I was thinking of leaving them with my friends or something...

Just Johnny

Letter from Johnny Akimoto to Ruth and Hideo, February 19, 1943 (Akimoto Family Collection)

Loyalty Questionnaire

Question #27 asked:

Are you willing to serve in the armed forces of the United States on combat duty, wherever ordered?

Question #28 asked:

Will you swear unqualified allegiance to the United States of America and faithfully defend the United States from any and all attack by foreign or domestic forces, and forswear any form of allegiance to the Japanese Emperor or any other foreign government, power, or organization?

Johnny's comments to his sister Ruth about the Loyalty Questionnaire reveal some of the humiliations the Japanese Americans had to endure. The questionnaire, designed to discern which Japanese Americans retained loyalty to Japan, infuriated the internees, adding insult to dishonor. The questionnaire proved divisive, as families became torn about whether their Constitutional rights were being violated again, whether their anger over internment should push loyal Japanese Americans to answer no to both questions as a protest, or whether eligible adults should join the same army that held their families captive. Those people who responded yes to these two questions were considered loyal. Individuals who responded no to one or both questions were considered disloyal, separated from their family, and sent to a more restrictive incarceration camp at Tule Lake, California.

Johnny, Victor, and Ted wanted to defend the country they loved. Despite the racial hatred and animosity they faced on a daily basis, the Akimoto brothers believed in the American dream. For them, the sacrifice of fighting for America would serve as an example and a reminder to future generations of true American patriotism.

Victor celebrated when he heard the announcement regarding the formation of an all-Japanese American combat regiment and applied for a transfer to join the unit at Camp Shelby, Mississippi. Promoted to sergeant, he transferred to the 442nd Regimental Combat Team on February 23, 1943. There, he joined the ranks of nearly 33,000 other soldiers of Japanese-American descent to fight for Uncle Sam.

A few weeks after Victor's arrival, Johnny made his way to Camp Shelby. Once there, Johnny took a few moments to write to his older sister, Ruth, to check on her.

AKIMOTO AND YASUDA WILL REPORT TO DENVER APRIL 6

Induction of the combat team volunteers in this center will begin April 6 and will continue until the 29th, according to a War department release received by Local Selective Service Board No. 35 at Lamar yesterday.

John Akimoto and Joe R. Yasuda are the first two Amache men to receive orders to report for induction. They must be in Denver on April 6.

The Lamar board reports that induction orders will be mailed to the volunteers as soon as their respective papers arrive from Washington and from the board at which they registered.

Papers have arrived for the following persons, who will receive their induction orders very shortly:

Kiyo Doiuchi, Peter S. Masuoka, Kazumi Kajioka, Yuki Akaki, George G. Tenimi, Tom Uyeda, A. Shin Sakamoto, Calvin T. Saito, Sam M. Takahashi, George Y. Shiino, Harry T. Kuwahara.

George S. Takeohi, Ben Sasaki, Yoshiro Befu, Mitsuma Yokohari, John K. Yamamoto, Robert Kashiwagi, Ichiro Kato, Masao Kawamoto, George Kashiwagi, Jack Mametsuka, Shoji Oniki.

CALENDAR

TODAY
7:00 p.m.--Movies, 12F mess hall.
7:30 p.m.--Senior high play, Terry hall.
7:30 p.m.--Movies, 12H mess hall.
7:30 p.m.--Japanese record hour, 7E mess hall.
TOMORROW
7:00 p.m.--Movies, 11H mess hall.
7:30 p.m.--Senior high play, Terry hall.
7:30 p.m.--Movies, 11K mess hall.
FRIDAY
7:00 p.m.--Movies, new picture, 9H mess hall.
7:30 p.m.--Movies, "Gunga Din," 9L mess hall.
7:30 p.m.--Senior high play, Terry hall.

COUNCIL MAKES REPLACEMENT

Granada Pioneer, March 31, 1943 (Courtesy of *Densho*)

May 13, 1943

Thurs. Nite

UNITED STATES ARMY
CAMP SHELBY, MISSISSIPPI

Dear Ruth,

Thanks an awful lot for the swell mittens. They'll sure come in handy.

How is everything coming along back in Idaho? I hope everything is working out OK.

It took me two weeks before I saw Vic. He was only across the street & I went over there about 4 or 5 times but he was attending school. He finally heard I was in so he came over.

All the fellows in my barracks are swell guys. The majority of them are from the islands [Hawaii]. Most of them are pretty disgusted with Mississippi. They said they would rather be back in the islands.

The company I'm in, is the heavy weapons infantry. That's machine guns and mortars. It's a pretty good outfit.

We started our basic training last Monday. From here on, it's going to be pretty tough. Tell Ted to start doing pushups and a lot of leg exercises cause he's going to have to jump right in with the rest of us.

Yesterday, we went on a little march but from now on, it's going to be a lot rougher.

Well, not much more to write about so I'll sign off.

Always,

Johnny

Letter from Johnny Akimoto to Ruth, May 13, 1943 (Akimoto Family Collection)

Victor (left) and Johnny Akimoto (right) at Camp Shelby, 1943 (Akimoto Family Collection)

Ted, Victor's second-youngest brother, was assigned to Camp Shelby a few weeks after Johnny. By the time he arrived, it quickly became clear that Victor had already made an impression on the Hawaiians gathered at Camp Shelby. Walking down the road, Ted came across a big Hawaiian soldier during his first week in camp. The Hawaiian said to Ted, "You Kotonk! You. Me. Fight!"

"Kotonk"

A derogatory nickname some Hawaiians called mainlanders. If a person was stupid enough, in a Hawaiian's opinion, to sit under a coconut tree and a coconut fell on their head, the sound it would make would be, "kotonk!"

It appeared that the Hawaiian wanted to fight Ted just for fun, as Hawaiians and mainlanders did not normally get along initially when they first arrived together in Camp Shelby.

They both took off their helmets and Ted, new to the Army way of life, prepared to get beaten to a pulp. Then the Hawaiian noticed the name inside Ted's helmet, "T. Akimoto" and said, "Victa you blah?"

Realizing the Hawaiian was asking about his brother Victor, Ted nodded his head. The Hawaiian put his helmet back on and said, "You okay. You me go eat."

When Victor transferred into the 100th Infantry Battalion, a Hawaiian unit of mostly-Japanese descent soldiers, they were already trained and prepared to go to the front lines. Upon arrival, he was challenged to a fight, to prove himself as a warrior. Tall and skinny, Victor seemed like easy pickings. But the Hawaiians had no way of knowing about Victor's life on the streets in Los Angeles. A Golden Gloves contender, who believed the Akimoto boys should know the basics of boxing, had given them weekly lessons.

The Hawaiian used huge, roundhouse punches. Victor kept him at a distance by constantly bobbing, jabbing, and hooking until the other soldier collapsed. The Hawaiian soldiers could not get over the fact that Victor had emerged victorious without a single, bloodletting blow smashing him to the ground. Thus, Victor saved Ted from a severe beating long before Ted even arrived at Camp Shelby.

Johnny, Jane, and Ted Akimoto, c. 1943 (Akimoto Family Collection)

Many of the mainland Japanese-American soldiers had very little money because they sent it to their families in the internment camps. The Hawaiian-born Japanese soldiers were invited to visit the nearby Japanese internment camp at Rohwer, Arkansas. Once they saw the conditions in the camps, the guard towers, and the barbed wire fences, they respected the mainlanders much more and the animosity between the groups subsided.

Victor, Johnny, and Ted were assigned to different infantry companies within the mostly Hawaiian 100th Infantry Battalion. Victor and Johnny both became infantrymen, foot soldiers. Ted trained as a communications sergeant assigned to the battalion headquarters.

As spring became summer in 1943, all three of the Akimoto brothers worried about their parents in the internment camp. Once they finished their training and duties for the day, they took time to write home. In this letter, Johnny mentions his brother-in-law, William "Bill" Kajikawa.

June 21, 1943

Monday night

UNITED STATES ARMY
CAMP SHELBY, MISSISSIPPI

Dear Mom & Pop,

I hope everything is OK up in Granada. We've been pretty busy with the two a days and didn't have much spare time. I saw Bill and Ted yesterday. Ted is in 1st Battalion Headquarters Company and Bill [Johnny's brother-in-law] is in the [522nd] Field Artillery.

I guess all of us are finally here. Only we're kinda split up.

There's really not much to write about so I'll sign off.

Take care of yourselves and please don't worry about us.

Always,

Johnny

Letter from Johnny Akimoto to his parents, June 21, 1943 (Akimoto Family Collection)

In March 1944, Johnny, the youngest of the brothers, received his orders to ship out to Italy. Victor and Ted's orders detailed their assignments to remain in the states and train new recruits.

The news of Johnny's orders to ship out shocked and infuriated Victor. He had promised his mother to keep Johnny and Ted safe. If Johnny were on a different continent, Victor would be unable to keep an eye on him. Victor went to the company chaplain for guidance. During World War II, company chaplains had a great deal of power and influence within the military. The chaplain spoke to the company commander on Victor's behalf, to seek alternate solutions.

Victor suggested that he could take Johnny's place on the front line, or that Johnny could be promoted to sergeant and remain in the states. Taking Victor aside, the commander explained the realities of war to him. Qualified sergeants, like Victor and his brother Ted, must train new recruits arriving in camp daily. Therefore, it would not be possible for Victor to trade places with Johnny. Nor would it be possible for Johnny to remain in the states as a sergeant. Infantry soldiers, men on the ground, were vital for success on the battlefields of Europe.

Victor then made the most important decision of his life. He proposed a new solution, a voluntary reduction in his own rank from sergeant to private. This way, he could join his brother Johnny overseas and the infantry would gain another soldier.

Impressed with Victor's patriotism and willingness to fight, the commander agreed to the proposal. Sergeant Akimoto became Private Victor Akimoto once again. Johnny and Ted, as well as the entire Akimoto family learned that Victor had sacrificed his own safety, possibly his life, to look out for his younger brother. He soon boarded the next Liberty ship headed to Italy to fight alongside Johnny.

Liberty Ship

Victory cargo ships lined up at a U.S. shipyard for loading of supplies, c. 1944 (*National Archives and Records Administration*)

The United States produced over 2,700 of these cargo and troop carriers during World War II. To produce such massive numbers of transports, 18 different shipyards employed thousands of workers including women, minorities, and veterans.

Entering Italy and Liberating Rome

Entering Italy and Liberating Rome are battle map interactives available on the ABMC website. These interactives allow you to better understand the campaigns, see historical photographs, and understand Allied troop movement.

Entering Italy **http://go.usa.gov/3AfyR**

Liberating Rome **http://go.usa.gov/3PpPP**

CHAPTER 8

Missing in Action, October 1944

As the stretcher bearers continued on their trek through the Vosges Mountains, Victor had to rely completely on the health and strength of others for his survival. Each POW faced a grim reality as captives of the enemy.

Daylight faded in the mountains as the exhausted American prisoners continued to struggle through the woods. Guns at their backs, arms and legs stretched to their limits, the GIs plodded onward. With each step away from the American lines, the chances of Victor's survival dwindled. The Germans marched him and the other newly acquired American POWs near the few surviving members of the 141st Infantry (the Lost Battalion) on their way back to the German lines. Once they finally arrived, the American POWs were separated into smaller sections by rank and condition. They prepared for transportation to prison camps throughout Germany and Poland.

The POWs clung to hope. With some luck, perhaps one of the members of their unit who escaped, like Second Lieutenant Young Oak Kim, had managed to notify command. Maybe a rescue team could liberate them.

Penicillin Joins the War

Young Oak Kim received one of the first doses of penicillin given to American soldiers. The new wonder drug, an antibiotic that cured bacterial infections, saved his life.

In any case, at least a "missing report" would be filed and their families notified.

Reports of Victor's capture, marked as confidential, were filed. The U.S. Army may not have wanted to answer questions about Victor's capture and that of the other American soldiers. Having to explain the violations of the Geneva Conventions concerning the use of the hospital flag with the red cross may not have been a conversation that the U.S. Army wanted to have with Victor's parents.

A missing report was filed on October 23, 1944. The army may have classified the report as confidential because of the circumstances of the Americans' capture. Additionally, the report may have been considered somewhat unreliable due to the medical condition of Second Lieutenant Kim, whose injuries very nearly claimed his life.

Classification ~~Removed~~

MISSING REPORT

Date: Jan. 4, 45

To accompany WD AGO Forms 66-1 or 74 of Missing or Missing in Action Personnel
(Other than those covered by Missing Air Crew Report.)

NAME AKIMOTO, Victor   ASN 19 078 557   GRADE Pvt   Arm or Service Inf

ORGN Co A 100th Bn, 442d Inf   APO 758   Date Reported MIA 23 Oct 44

MISSION Being evacuated to the rear aid station

POINT OF DEPARTURE Biffontaine, France   DATE 23 Oct 44

INTENDED DESTINATION Bn Aid Station, V295576

LAST KNOWN WHEREABOUTS V312582, Map, Eastern France, Bruyeres, 1/50,000

BRIEF RESUME OF CIRCUMSTANCES SURROUNDING DISAPPEARANCE:

Pvt Akimoto, 19078557, was a litter case and he was being evacuated to the rear aid
station with several other wounded soldiers. Apparently this group lost their way
in the thickly wooded area and ran into an enemy patrol. The entire group were
presumably captured with the exception of a few who escaped.

STATEMENTS OF WITNESSES, IF ANY:

REMARKS: (Any information not covered above, including details and results of
search, if any, conducted)

Enlisted Branch ppl
Week?
Coc Br. 4
B. Maids

Date of Report 2 Nov 44

(Signature of preparing officer)
ALBERT A. KOBY
WOJG USA, 442d Inf
Asst Adj

Determined to be an
Administrative Marking
Not National Security Information
By ___ NARA Date 1/7/15

Missing Report, U.S. Army War Department, November 1944 (*U.S. Army*)

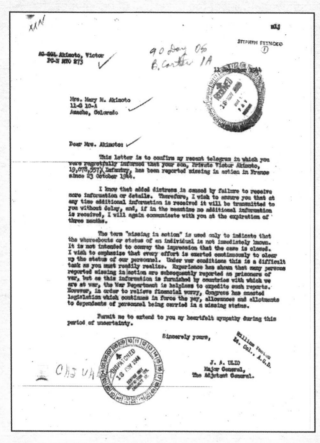

Missing in Action Letter, U.S. Army War Department, November 1944 (*U.S. Army*)

For whatever reasons: a misplaced report, confidentiality, or the complicated nature of trying to win the largest war in history, Mary and Masanori Akimoto were not notified about Victor's injuries nor his capture. The War Department sent a telegram on November 10 and a letter on November 11 to Mrs. Akimoto at the internment camp, notifying her that Victor was missing in action.

Back at the border between Germany and France, Victor was given a better understanding of the full extent of his injuries. The bullet had fractured his thigh bone, the impact causing his right knee joint to separate.

When the Germans divided the captured soldiers, Victor was separated from healthy American POWs and transferred to a German military hospital. He arrived at the military hospital at Seligenstadt, Germany, on or about October 28, 1944, nearly 200 miles away from Biffontaine, France.

The American medics had managed to stop the bleeding and bandage his leg. The limited amount of morphine, given to him to help reduce the pain from the shattered bone, had long worn off. His clothing remained dirty. For Victor, the pain, blood loss, lack of food, and poor clothing became minor concerns. A much more serious threat loomed on the horizon: infection.

—— **CHAPTER NINE** ——

ITALY, 1944

In early 1944, Johnny and Victor landed on beaches near Anzio, Italy. This battle would prove critical to the southern European campaign for the Allies due to its close proximity to Rome. The Allies wanted to capitalize on recent victories in North Africa by pressuring the Axis in southern Europe. By doing so, the Allies could prepare for a full-scale invasion in the summer of 1944 through France. Additionally, the assault on Italy would help reduce the tremendous battering the Russians were experiencing on the Eastern front.

World War II (Interactive Timeline)

If you are interested in learning more about World War II, visit:

http://go.usa.gov/3AfV9

The battle for Anzio erupted in January 1944 and lasted nearly five months. Johnny and Victor replaced injured or killed soldiers. The coastal terrain proved terrible for attacking an enemy. The Allied troops became bogged down in the vast muddy marshlands, while German troops targeted them from the surrounding hills. American commanders worried about their troops becoming entrenched as had happened during World War I. Anzio became a brutal battleground, with nearly 40,000 Allied casualties, including 7,000 killed and 33,000 wounded or missing in action.

Company guidon bearers of the 100th Infantry Battalion, c. 1944 (*National Archives and Records Administration*)

In their letters home from Italy, Johnny and Victor lied about the realities of war to spare their family pain and worry. Of course, all letters from the front were censored, since captured letters could reveal sensitive information to the Germans such as unit sizes and strength, supply lines, and future battle plans. Instead, soldiers often focused on issues at home. In one letter, Johnny expressed his displeasure about his parents' mistreatment in Idaho. Writing from a hospital bed in Italy, he wrote to his sister Ruth:

AMERICAN RED CROSS

March 22, 1944

Dear Ruth,

Them Idaho farmers reacted just as I thought they would. I like to be back there and break a few of their noses. I only wish I could have them under me for a month. That would be the worst month they'd ever have.

What have they to yell about? They didn't get evacuated, they're making good money and everybody else is getting drafted so why should they get deferred? Back there, they don't feel the war except they're making money. I hope the whole slew of them get taken in.

I guess you know that we're somewhere in Italy but get a laugh at this. I've been in the hospital for the past two weeks. Now don't get excited—it's not what you think—it's mumps! I couldn't get it in the states but as soon as I come over here it gets me. Kinda burns me up. One consolation thou, the nurses here are really swell and taking life real easy. In fact, too easy. Doesn't seem like the army. –Johnny.

Letter from Johnny Akimoto to Ruth, March 22, 1944 (Akimoto Family Collection)

Meanwhile, Ted Akimoto remained stranded in the states. His headquarters company received orders to send a detail of men for a short, special assignment. Ted guarded German prisoners of war going to and from farm details, and stood watch at night. When another detail of men traveled by train to Ocala, Florida, Ted became an actor in an army training film. They stayed in nice hotels, ate in fancy restaurants and because it was a War Department job, the hotel received extra ration points. Everyone ate steaks. Another group of soldiers assigned to the training film, veterans from battlefields of Alaska, had fought to recapture two islands, Attu and Kiska on the Aleutian Island chain, from the Japanese.

During the filming, Ted and the other Japanese American soldiers marched in the background of one scene because no one could tell they were Asian. Ted later donned the uniform of the Japanese Army and went to Silver Springs, Florida, where he portrayed a Japanese sniper, sneaking through the jungle and then a dead body on a sand dune. All these surreal experiences could not diminish the constant fear and knowledge that his two brothers were still in danger overseas, or dampen his desperate desire to join them as soon as possible.

Ration Points

During World War II, items such as sugar, butter, meat, and gasoline became limited. To make sure everyone received their fair share, the U.S. Government issued ration books or tokens, which allowed the bearer to purchase a limited quantity of the rationed items.

When the film crew found out Ted had experience as a photographer, they handed him a camera and he started taking still photos. All in all, while his brothers were in combat in Italy, it was a cushy two weeks for Ted in Florida.

CHAPTER TEN

JOHNNY WILL NEVER COME MARCHING HOME, 1944

Victor and Johnny maintained contact throughout the battles of Anzio, where Johnny earned a Bronze Star for heroism or meritorious service in connection with a military operation. Occasionally, Johnny would write quick notes meant to put his parents' minds at ease. This postcard, dated July 12, 1944, arrived at the Amache Internment Camp after August 20, 1944.

Front side of postcard, July 12, 1944 (Akimoto Family Collection)

July 12, 1944

Dear folks,

Just dropping a letter to let you know I'm okay and everything is fine. Please don't worry about us and take good care of each other and we hope to be home in the near future. Give my regards to all and hope you all are in good health. – Johnny[5]

Postcard from Johnny Akimoto to his parents, July 12, 1944 (Akimoto Family Collection)

On July 30, 1944, Johnny checked into a military field hospital in Italy suffering from a severe stomach ache, which was soon diagnosed as acute hepatitis. He had contracted the infection from an unknown source in Italy.

Normally, the liver cleanses the blood of impurities and toxins. When the deadly hepatitis virus attacked Johnny's liver, it created a condition in which the vital organ could not breakdown bilirubin, a toxic compound produced from the cleaning of red blood cells that transport fresh oxygen to the body. The excess bilirubin caused Johnny's skin, eyes, and mucus membranes in his mouth to turn yellowish in color, a condition known as jaundice. The infection also resulted in a fever of over 102 degrees. The infection began to take over his internal organs. On August 1, Johnny's liver failed and he slipped into a coma. At 4 a.m. on August 2, 1944, Johnny died.

The War Department sent a telegram within two weeks to Masanori Akimoto at Amache. Dated August 18, 1944 the telegram notified him of his son's death.

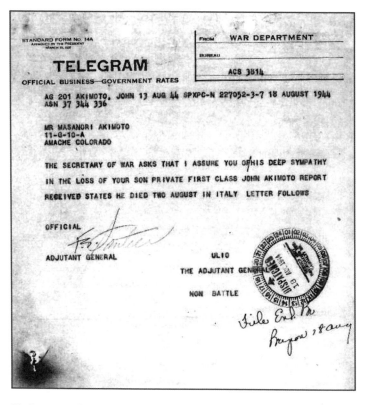

War Department Telegram to Masanori Akimoto, August 18, 1944 (*U.S. Army*)

Days later, on August 21, 1944, the War Department sent a longer explanation to Masanori and Mary, with details of Johnny's passing.

The Akimoto family was devastated. Mary and Masanori tried to cope with the deprivations of internment camp life along with the loss of their youngest son, Johnny.

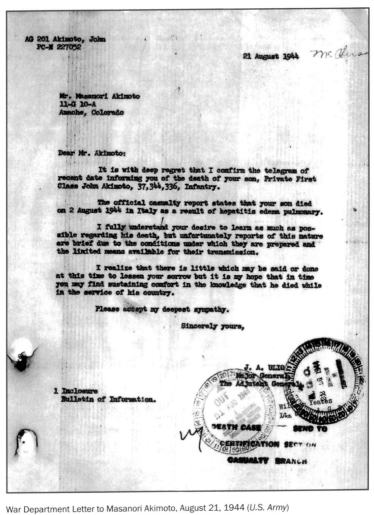

AG 201 Akimoto, John
PC-N 227052

21 August 1944

Mr. Masanori Akimoto
11-G 10-A
Amache, Colorado

Dear Mr. Akimoto:

It is with deep regret that I confirm the telegram of
recent date informing you of the death of your son, Private First
Class John Akimoto, 37,344,336, Infantry.

The official casualty report states that your son died
on 2 August 1944 in Italy as a result of hepatitis edema pulmonary.

I fully understand your desire to learn as much as possible regarding his death, but unfortunately reports of this nature
are brief due to the conditions under which they are prepared and
the limited means available for their transmission.

I realize that there is little which may be said or done
at this time to lessen your sorrow but it is my hope that in time
you may find sustaining comfort in the knowledge that he died while
in the service of his country.

Please accept my deepest sympathy.

Sincerely yours,

J. A. ULIO
Major General,
The Adjutant General.

1 Inclosure
Bulletin of Information.

War Department Letter to Masanori Akimoto, August 21, 1944 (*U.S. Army*)

Ted Akimoto, who received a copy of the same telegram, remained
in the U.S. In Silver Springs, Florida, he wrote to his parents to try to
help them understand Johnny's passion for fighting in the war:

68

CAMERA CREW #9
GENERAL DELIVERY
SILVER SPRINGS, FLA.
SUNDAY —

DEAR DAD + MOMS,

I RECEIVED YOUR TELEGRAM TODAY AFTER WORK. PLEASE BELIEVE ME, IT CAME AS JUST AS MUCH A SHOCK TO ME AS IT MUST HAVE BEEN TO YOU.

I WENT TO SEE THE MINISTER OF THE EPISCOPAL CHURCH IN TOWN AND HAD HIM SAY A FEW WORDS OF PRAYER FOR JOHNNY, AFTER WHICH HE TALKED TO ME FOR A WHILE. HE MADE ME FEEL CONSIDERABLY BETTER.

I NEVER TOLD YOU THIS BEFORE AS I THOUGHT IT WOULD BE BAD LUCK TO MENTION IT, BUT, JUST BEFORE JOHNNY EMBARKED, HE SAID: "IF I DON'T HAPPEN TO COME BACK, TELL EVERYONE, ESPECIALLY MOM, TO NOT CRY TOO MUCH BECAUSE THERE'S ENOUGH SADNESS IN THIS WORLD ALREADY, OKAY?" SO I LAUGHED AND TOLD HIM NOT TO TALK SO CRAZY, BUT SAID "OKAY". HOWEVER TONIGHT, I WENT UP TO MY ROOM AND CRIED LIKE A BABY FOR ABOUT AN HOUR. I JUST COULDN'T HELP IT. SO CRY MOM, BUT DON'T GRIEVE TOO LONG. I KNOW THAT JOHNNY DIED HAPPY, AMONG HIS FRIENDS, AND KNOWING THAT HE WAS FIGHTING TO MAKE A BETTER PLACE FOR CHILDREN SUCH AS JON AND MARGARET'S BABY TO COME. WE USED TO TALK ABOUT IT A LOT WHEN WE WERE IN SHELBY TOGETHER. NO MATTER WHAT THE COST, WE HAVE TO MAKE THIS WORLD A BETTER PLACE FOR THE COMING GENERATIONS SO THAT THEY WON'T HAVE TO GO THROUGH THE TRIALS AND TRIBULATIONS

69

AIR MAIL

THE "NIHONJINS" HAVE HAD TO GO THROUGH UP TO
NOW. — SO JOHNNY HAS GIVEN HIS "ALL" TO
WHAT HE FIRMLY BELIEVED IN, AND WHAT I ALSO
BELIEVE IN. — THIS IS AS HE WOULD HAVE WANTED
IT, THAT MUCH I AM SURE.

I HOPE I HAVE HELPED, DAD & MOM TO GIVE YOU
SOME IDEA OF HOW JOHNNY FELT AND HOW I
NOW FEEL. CAN'T SAY MORE.

LOVE
Ted.

SGT TED AKIMOTO 39915052
CAMERA CREW #9
GENERAL DELIVERY
SILVER SPRINGS, FLORIDA

OCALA
AUG 21
10 00 AM
1944
FLA

VIA AIR MAIL

MR + MRS. M. AKIMOTO
11 G - 10A
GRANADA
COLORADO .

about Johnny's death

Letter from Ted Akimoto to his parents, August 21, 1944 (Akimoto Family Collection)

70

Meanwhile, still fighting northward through Italy, Victor also struggled to deal with Johnny's death. In the following letter, Victor attempts to explain the confusion regarding Johnny's death to his parents. Throughout the letter Victor hints at the responsibility he feels for his younger siblings. He describes the circumstances and chronology of Johnny's death. More important, Victor articulates a vision for why he and Johnny chose to fight so passionately on shores so far away from home.

September 4, 1944

Italy

Dearest Mother & Dad,

I received your letter today in which you stated that the War Dept. had sent you a telegram notifying you that John had passed away on the 2nd. I can readily understand why you were puzzled when my letter dated the 3rd and Bill's letter dated July 30th had stated that John was alright. The reason for that was that Bill came to see me on the 30th and I told him that John had complained of a stomachache and that he had gone to the hospital but none of us thought it was serious. As our company pulled out on a special detail the next morning, I didn't have any knowledge of John's passing away until six days later when a good friend of mine in C Company hitch-hiked to our company 25 miles away to inform me of the sad news.

As soon as I heard the shocking news I went to the Medics and John's old company to find out the details.

According to the report John went to the hospital on the 30th (of July) and it seems he had acute liver trouble and that he passed away before they had a chance to operate.

I see that John's loss has hit the whole family hard and am very sorry to hear that Mother took sick. As in my last letter it's hard to express my feelings but coming over on the boat John and I used to talk about home a lot. One of the things we agreed on was neither of us had the slightest fear of death and so if it was God's will that we should give our lives to our country, we wanted you folks to be proud and not mourn; for this is the greatest cause a man can give his life for, as we are fighting on the side of God. As for me, I am in the best of health and please don't worry about my safety as I am in the best company of this battalion.

From the news we received of our troops in France it looks as if victory should come within the very near future so who knows we might be home for Christmas dinner yet. So you folks please take good care of yourselves and don't worry about Bill[6] or me for we really see very little action now days. I have to close now so please tell Mother I am praying for her quick recovery.

Love,

Vic

Letter from Victor Akimoto to his parents, September 4, 1944 (Akimoto Family Collection)

Johnny was buried with military honors at the U.S. military cemetery in Vada, Italy. A temporary cross marked his grave at Plot A, Row 12, Grave 142.

Mary became ill after learning of Johnny's death. Knowing that Victor remained in perilous danger did not help. Fear, anger, and despair hung over the heads of the Akimotos as Victor continued to fight.

CHAPTER ELEVEN

Wounded POW, November 1944

After his capture, Victor was transported to Germany by truck. The exhausting trip took everything out of Victor. He arrived in very poor condition at the German military hospital near Seligenstadt, which means Blessed City in English.

As October gave way to November, Victor continued to hope that the Americans would break through the German lines and rescue him. His fight for survival became a daily chore. His leg wound, debrided and cleaned by the American medics in France, needed constant attention.

Debriding a Wound

The unhealthy tissue around the wound is removed and sterilized with iodine or another disinfectant to reduce the chance of infection.

Nearby, on a wooded hilltop, was Stalag IX-B POW Camp (also known as Bad Orb), for enlisted soldiers. The hospital at Bad Orb had limited capabilities with two American doctors who treated hundreds of soldiers as best as they could. The camp was notorious for its deplorable living conditions. In early December, as his condition worsened, Victor was transferred from the Seligenstadt hospital to Bad Orb for more treatment.

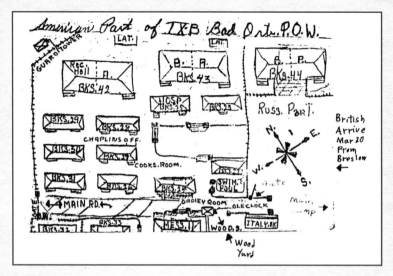

Map of Prisoner of War Camp Stalag IX-B, Bad Orb, Germany, 1945. The hospital was located in barrack 25. (Courtesy of www.IndianaMilitary.org and Pete House)

Victor clung to life at Bad Orb. Without antibiotics, sulfa powder and pills, proper sterilization and medical supplies, first the German, then the American doctors struggled to properly treat his injury. The destruction to the bones, soft tissues, and skin should have been surgically repaired at a proper first aid station or hospital facility. Those procedures were most likely not available to Victor. With each passing day in the prisoner of war camp, Victor's body struggled to fight against persistent infections.

On Valentine's Day 1945, Masanori and Mary Akimoto wrote to the War Department trying to get some answers about their lost son.

11G – 10A
Amache, Colorado
February 14, 1945
War Department
The Adj. Generals Office
Washington, D.C.

Re: A G 201 Akimoto, Victor

PC – N InJO 273

Dear Sirs:

It has been over three months since your telegram of November 10th and your letter of November 11th in regards to our son, Victor (19078557) who has been missing in action since October 23rd. We lost one son, John in Italy on August 2, 1944 so you can well understand why we are anxious to get some information about Victor.

According to your letter you stated that you would communicate with us again after the expiration of three months. Since we haven't heard from you we are writing to see if you have been able to obtain any further information.

Could you please let us know at the earliest possible time?

Thank you.

Sincerely,
Mr. & Mrs. M. Akimoto

Letter written by Mr. and Mrs. Akimoto to the War Department, February 14, 1945 (Akimoto Family Collection)

The War Department never responded to the Akimotos' plea for information. While Mary, Masanori, and the rest of the Akimoto family waited for word about Victor, the U.S. Army was recovering from a deadly German offensive, the Battle of the Bulge, and pressing toward Germany to win the largest war in human history, World War II.

Chapter Twelve

Victor in Italy and France, 1944

Allied Military Advance through Italy, 1943–1944

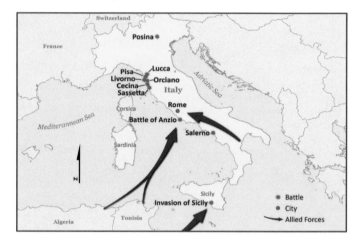

Allied forces landed in Sicily (Operation Husky) in July 1943 and Salerno (Operation Avalanche) in September 1943. The forces pushed north, and Rome fell on June 5, 1944 (Peter Koby).

Victor remained with A Company of the 100th Infantry Battalion after Johnny's death. His company earned the nickname the "Purple Heart Battalion" for their heroic deeds and casualties suffered in battle. The company's motto, "Remember Pearl Harbor!" became "Go For Broke!" when they joined forces with the rest of the 442nd Regimental Combat Team from Camp Shelby. That slogan came to define the fighting attitude of the Japanese-American troops.

The 100th Infantry Battalion helped to destroy the large German artillery south of Rome. However, these same Japanese-American troops were not allowed to go to Rome – the Caucasian troops

442nd Regimental Combat Team shoulder patch, c. 1943. (Akimoto Family Collection)

rolled into Rome instead. Due to racial tensions in the states, the generals decided it would not look good to have Japanese-American soldiers riding victoriously through Rome.

After Rome was liberated, the 100th Infantry Battalion was assigned to the 442nd Regimental Combat Team. The 100th Infantry Battalion became the 1st Battalion of the 442nd. Each American infantry regiment or regimental combat team had three battalions during World War II. This often caused confusion because the soldiers of the 100th Infantry Battalion continued to identify with their original unit through the rest of the war. At times, the men of the 442nd Regimental Combat Team used both designations interchangeably. However, the official U.S. Army designation is the 1st Battalion, 442nd Regimental Combat Team (RCT).

After Anzio, Victor fought through a series of battles including Hill 415, Belvedere, Sassetta, Cecina, Castellina, Postina, Orciano, Livorno, Pisa, and Lucca.

Huge battles occurred throughout Italy. Victor was just one individual in an Allied front that absorbed massive amounts of resources and soldiers. Victor's battalion continued moving through Italy amassing more Purple Hearts, Medals of Honor, and Presidential Unit Citations than any other unit in American history—a record that remains unbroken to this day.

In one battle, Victor became separated from his weapon. Perhaps he ran out of ammo or his gun jammed, but he found himself in a perilous situation. He frantically searched the area for another weapon when he came across four armed Germans. Somehow, Victor convinced the Germans that he had the upper hand, and they surrendered. For capturing four Germans without a weapon, he was awarded a Bronze Star.

On June 6, 1944, the Allies made their famous landing at Normandy in France. Meanwhile, Victor's unit, after completing their assignments in Italy, traveled to Naples for a brief period of rest and relaxation, then on to Marseille, France, to begin a direct northward assault on Germany. General Dwight D. Eisenhower's plan was to crush the Germans between the hammer of the Normandy landings and the anvil of troops moving north after Operation Dragoon landed in southern France in August 1944. When the two armies met up, they would attack Germany on a massive front along the German border. Victor's unit traveled up the Rhone River Valley by train and then on foot until they approached the forests on the border between France and Germany.

Supreme Commander of Allied Troops in Europe, General Dwight D. Eisenhower led the coalition of Allied forces though the European theatre during World War II. In 1953, he became president of the United States of America. (*Naval History and Heritage Command*)

Allied Military Strategy in Western Europe, 1943–1944

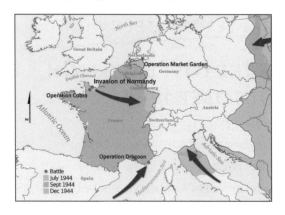

The goal of the Allied advance was to join forces of the Hammer–the Normandy Invasion, Operation Cobra, and the push to capture Berlin–with the Anvil–the invasion of Italy and Operation Dragoon. The goal was that Allied forces would meet in eastern France and advance across the Rhine River into Germany. (Peter Koby)

Normandy

If you are interested in learning more about the landings at the Normandy Beaches, visit: **http://go.usa.gov/3AfVT**

CHAPTER THIRTEEN

BATTLE OF THE LOST BATTALION, OCTOBER 1944

As fall became winter in central Europe, the world braced for the final European battles of World War II. By the time the 442nd Regimental Combat Team arrived at France's Vosges Mountains, the fighting was frantic. Adolf Hitler had ordered his troops to fight to the last man to defend Germany from the Allied advance.

Victor's company would be fighting in mountain terrain, much trickier than the flat plains of Italy. Here, they had to contend with trees, rocks, fog, and rain, as well as a highly trained, professional German Army fighting to defend its homeland.

442nd Regimental Combat Team members at the Battle of the Lost Battalion, October 1944 (*U.S. Army Signal Corps*)

The 442nd Regimental Combat Team was ordered to rescue the 141st Infantry Regiment, composed of members mostly from Texas. Allied bombers air-dropped supplies to the surviving 275 Texans. But the weather conditions were so poor that most of the supplies fell into German hands. Artillery shells stuffed with emergency supplies, aimed at the entrenched Americans, fell into enemy hands as well.

The 442nd Regimental Combat Team battled for days before finally breaking through the German defenses. On October 30, 230 men of the 141st Infantry Regiment came out alive. The 442nd suffered over 800 casualties, deaths and injuries combined. More Japanese-American soldiers sacrificed and lost their lives in what became known as the Battle of the Lost Battalion than soldiers of the 141st Infantry Regiment were saved.[7] When the dead and injured were counted, the 442nd Regimental Combat Team lost over three times more soldiers than they saved.

A week and a half after the battle, on November 12, 1944, the 442nd stood in formation for review by General John E. Dahlquist, one of the officers in charge of the Battle of the Lost Battalion. Standing in the snow, the soldiers lined up in parade formation behind their flags.

As General Dahlquist came to K Company, one unit of the 442ⁿᵈ Regimental Combat Team, he noticed there were only 18 soldiers in formation. Speaking to the officer in charge of K Company, Lieutenant Colonel Miller, Dahlquist shouted, "I want all of your men to stand for this formation!" Miller replied, "That's all of K Company left, sir." K Company had started with 400 men. By the end, only 18 men remained capable of standing.*

The color guard of the 442ⁿᵈ Regimental Combat Team stands at attention on the frozen fields near Bruyeres, France, November 1944 (*U.S. Army Center of Military History*)

* See Epilogue Pages 128–129

CHAPTER FOURTEEN

Amputation, December 1944

As relentless as time, the weather outside Victor's hospital bed moved from fall to winter. By mid-December, Victor's worst nightmares were coming true. Constant fever, lack of mobility, and a wound that refused to heal reduced his chances of survival.

His infected wound continued to worsen and turned to gangrene. Victor's sepsis infection started the moment his skin was ruptured by the German bullet. The contamination started locally and then spread via his bloodstream. Over the weeks, his blood started to carry infectious bacteria to his major organs. His organs became unable to cope with the toxic blood supply and the ability of his body to clean toxins decreased. Eventually, his organs would begin to shut down.

Sepsis Infection

A sepsis infection usually starts with the rupture of the skin. Bacteria attack the wound and then spread via the bloodstream to other parts of the body including the major organs.

Gangrene

The cells of the tissues around a wound die because they have a reduced supply of healthy red blood cells. Dead tissue cells, in turn, become part of the infection.

The doctors determined Victor would not survive unless the sepsis infection was stopped. They decided to amputate Victor's leg above the knee. By removing the lower half of the limb, they hoped he would be able to fight off the infection.

Victor now faced having his leg removed while still conscious. Anesthetics allow doctors to put patients to sleep and to conduct operations without causing pain to the patient. However, these drugs were probably not available for Victor or any other POW, since Germany reserved medical supplies for soldiers and civilians, not Allied prisoners of war.

Other POWs held down Victor's shoulders, torso, and legs during the procedure. Victor bit down on a stick while the doctors sawed through his thigh tissues and bone.

After the procedure, Victor recovered enough to speak to his doctor. He had just one request: no more food.

Amputation

An amputation is the removal of a limb, arm or leg. The surgical procedure is done to increase the chances of survival of the patient.

CHAPTER FIFTEEN

TED GOES TO JAPAN, 1945

With Victor's whereabouts unknown and Johnny already dead, Ted agonized over his lost brothers. Despite his best efforts to join the battle overseas, Ted seemed stymied by endless bureaucracy. He was finally offered the opportunity to attend Officer Candidate School (OCS), the only viable route left that might possibly afford the chance of an overseas deployment to search for Victor. A letter from his friend George Harada, who was then fighting overseas, reminded him again that he remained stateside.

V-Mail

During World War II, many letters to and from frontline soldiers were sent via V-Mail. The original letter was censored, photographed, placed onto microfilm, and reprinted on paper at the other end. Thus, 37 bags of mail with 150,000 one-page letters could be sent in one sack.

TO: T/Sgt. Ted Akimoto 39915052
HQ and HQ Co, 171 Inf BN (Sep)
Camp Shelby, MISS

From: Pfc. G. Harada, 39168082
Co D, 100 NB, 442 Inf Reg't
APO 758, C/O P.M, NY. NY.

28 Feb. 1945

Dear Ted:

It appears, finally, that the brass hats [officers] in your outfit have come to their senses by sending you to OCS [Officer Candidate School]. Believe me, pal, if guys such as Sad Sack and Fat Boy could make the grade, it's only common justice that you be given the same chance. Frankly, I think you'll make a corking good officer, Ted, and I'm all for it. It's rather odd too, for Tumabashi and I were beating our gums just before your V-mail came, and I mentioned that you must have gone to OCS, or something since you hadn't written in sometime. We both agreed that such an event would bring up considerably the average of the officer corp [sic] in your battalion. So, go to it, son.

There's a dearth of news lately for we've been doing a great deal of nothing, which of course, doesn't hurt my feelings at all. On the other hand it does make letter writing difficult! Of course, I could dwell upon the scenic wonders of France, but I'm sure you wouldn't care for that.

Regarding that picture you saw, it was taken in Italy nearly a year ago (how time passes!) a few miles north of Cisterna, on the Road to Rome. To give you an idea of how the so-called "combat photographer" works, it was taken some 5 or 6 miles behind the front lines. Incidentally, the guy in the front of me is Dochin, your brother Johnny's pal. I remember the day as being torrid and dusty, for the unpaved road had been ground down to a fine powder some 4 or 5 inches deep, and each step would add to the stifling cloud that we raised as we passed.

Yeah, Ted, I'd appreciate a copy of the Reader [sic] Digest and also the Infantry Journal of December that I mentioned previously. Can it be arranged?

Take things easy Ted – that is until you hit Benning. I'll be rooting for you pal —

Your buddy,

George

Letter from George Harada to Ted Akimoto, February 28, 1945 (Akimoto Family Collection)

Assigned to the Infantry Training Center at Fort McClellan, Alabama, after training at Fort Benning, Georgia, Ted made inquiries about a reassignment to combat with the 442[nd.]

When a company clerk told Ted he had new orders, he leapt at the opportunity. To his surprise, he was sent to the Japanese Language School in Fort Snelling, Minnesota.

For 30 days, 10 hours a day, seven days a week, Ted had to memorize interrogation questions in Japanese such as, "You're lying! Who is your commanding officer? Where did you hide your weapons?" Then he learned the words for regiment, battalion, machine guns, and numbers—nothing he could use in normal conversation. Ironically, Ted, who learned very little Japanese, took command of 120 Nisei translators and interpreters who could speak, read, and write Japanese fluently in preparation for his next assignment, Japan. All the while, Ted hoped for news that Victor was alive and safe.

On May 8, 1945, Nazi Germany gave its unconditional surrender and ended hostilities in Europe. Ted, in July 1945, departed on a train from Minnesota to Seattle on a cross-country trip through southern Idaho. He was being deployed to Japan.

As the train paused at 2 a.m. at an isolated train station near Mountain Home, Idaho, Ted noticed one of his soldiers jump off the train. The young man ran to his girlfriend, hugged her, kissed her, and then re-boarded the train. The young woman returned to the Minidoka Internment Camp.

After Ted and his troops arrived in Seattle to prepare for the invasion of Japan, it rained straight for nearly 20 days. His company repeatedly practiced emergency drills: climbing up and down the rope cargo ladders in case they were struck by a torpedo. On August 6 and August 9, respectively,

Hiroshima and Nagasaki

The atomic bombs dropped by the United States on these two cities killed between 100,000 and 240,000 people. Hundreds of thousands more were injured or contracted illnesses from the radiation. These are the only nuclear weapons to ever have been used in warfare.

the U.S. dropped atomic bombs on Hiroshima and Nagasaki. Just before Ted's unit departed the port, Imperial Japan surrendered on August 14, 1945, the war in the Pacific came to a close and ended all combat in World War II.

The invasion of Japan was canceled, sparing Ted and thousands of other American soldiers the perils of an assault on the Japanese islands. The dropping of the atomic bombs and the impending invasion by the Soviet Union forced Japan to surrender. However Ted's unit still shipped out, navigated through the tail end of a typhoon, and docked in Yokohama.

Photograph of Generals Douglas MacArthur (left) and Dwight D. Eisenhower (right) by Ted Akimoto, c. 1945 (Akimoto Family Collection)

Immediately, Ted knew that war impacted the people of Yokohama. The streets, lined with poorly dressed children without shoes, smelled of burnt timbers and foul water. Buildings and whole sections of the city appeared demolished and destroyed by the American bombing raids. Ted and other soldiers grabbed whatever they could carry from the ship, including candy, food, clothing, and medical supplies for the Japanese civilians. They began distributing necessities as they traveled through the smoldering cities. Being a military intelligence officer in charge of a team of translators, with no Japanese language skills himself, Ted sought new opportunities.

Surrender of Japan

General Douglas MacArthur signed the formal surrender agreement on-board the U.S.S. *Missouri*. Standing behind General MacArthur are Lieutenant General Jonathan Wainwright, survivor of the Bataan Death March and three years in Japanese Prisoner of War Camps, and British Lieutenant General A. E. Percival, also a POW of the Japanese. *(National Archives and Records Administration)*

When word reached Ted that the Army Signal Corps needed a photographer, he dropped everything and drove a jeep to Tokyo. His experience as a high school photography club member paid off when he landed a job as one of General Douglas MacArthur's photographers.

Using MacArthur's personal plane Ted took photos of Mount Fuji, the eruption of Mount Aso, and some of the first photos of the devastation of Hiroshima. During his

Radiation Danger

The dangers of exposure to atomic radiation were not widely known in 1945. Countless people died of issues related to radiation exposure.

time as a photographer for the Army, Ted and his team were also ordered to document the devastating effects of the atomic bombs, including the horrendous damage to surviving radiation victims.

Ted Akimoto and General Tansey's secretary (name unknown) 50 yards from ground zero in Hiroshima, 1945 (Akimoto Family Collection)

Chapter Sixteen

Bad Orb, January 1945

By early January 1945, living conditions of the camp started to deteriorate exponentially for prisoners at Bad Orb. The Battle of the Bulge, launched by the Germans on December 16, 1944, caught the POW camp commanders off guard. Overnight, thousands of Allied POWs were crammed into the camps. Food, clothing, shelter, medicine, and supplies of all types were in short supply.

When the International Red Cross visited the Bad Orb camp on January 24, 1945, conditions were terrible. Most of the prisoners arrived at the freezing end of December 1944 from the Western front. Captured in battles in Luxembourg, Belgium, and France, the average prisoner took nine days to arrive at the camp. The German authorities, unprepared for the sudden arrival of 1,500 men, forced the POWs to sleep on crowded, bare wooden floors in barracks with missing or broken windows.

Upon arrival, the men were de-loused with chemicals and given a hot bath. The camp commandant, Oberst Seiber, told Red Cross officials that Bad Orb was a temporary camp and the bulk of the prisoners would be moved to other locations. In several barracks, lights, washing facilities, and toilets remained unavailable. Appalling conditions existed in the few indoor and outdoor latrines.

Berga Concentration Camp

To make room in Bad Orb after the Battle of the Bulge in January of 1945, 350 Jewish American POWs were pulled out and marched north to the Berga Concentration Camp. Most of the transferred POWs constructed underground tunnels for armament factories 12 hours a day, seven days a week. Without masks to filter the dust, coats or adequate footwear, the American POW casualty rates at Berga became much higher than at other POW camps. Near the end of the war some of the prisoners, forced on death marches by the Nazis to avoid liberation, barely survived.

If you are interested in learning more about Berga, visit: **http://www.pbs.org/ wnet/berga/**

Jewish American POWs at Berga Concentration Camp, 1945 (*National Archives and Record Administration*)

Members of the visiting International Red Cross delegation noted that most prisoners had a German blanket for warmth. Yet the thin blankets had holes or large sections of threadbare material, and 30 men had no blankets at all. In the middle of the German winter, some men possessed only underclothing with a shirt and trousers. Many had no boots to protect their feet from frostbite; nearly one-fifth of the men had no coats.

By mid-February each prisoner had sent his "first card" to relatives at home, to inform them of their whereabouts. According to the Geneva Conventions, POWs were allowed to write home to their families. The lack of stationary, cards, and writing utensils remained a sore point with the prisoners.

Throughout that cold winter, Mary and Masanori Akimoto anxiously waited for word concerning Victor. Notecards were completed at the camp detailing Victor's condition, but Mary never received any of these communications at Amache. Neither his parents nor the U.S. Army received word about Victor from him or the German authorities.

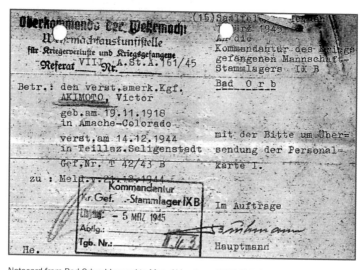

Notecard from Bad Orb addressed to Mary Akimoto, c. 1945 (*U.S. Army*)

On February 9, 1945, a telegram sent to the U.S. Secretary of State by the Red Cross raised more alarm bells about the soldiers at Bad Orb. By mid-March 1945, problems had reached critical status according to the International Committee of the Red Cross.

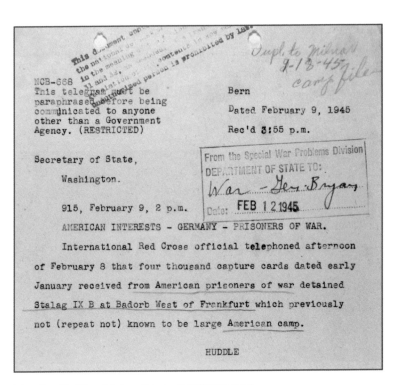

International Red Cross Telegram, February 9, 1945 (*U.S. Army*)

The prisoners evacuated ahead of the Russian advance on the eastern front arrived at Bad Orb in deplorable condition. Many of the POWs arrived suffering from frostbite, considerable loss of weight, dysentery, diarrhea, hemorrhagic fever, and general pneumonia. Hygiene was nonexistent, vermin swarmed the camp, and many of the POWs had only shreds of clothing left. Reports of typhoid outbreaks circulated. The severely overcrowded barracks and emergency tents in muddy fields forced many of the prisoners to sleep on dirty floors. Food rations dwindled to meager portions, and the camp lacked salt, a nutritional necessity, for several weeks.

Finally, on April 2, 1945, elements of the 2nd Infantry Battalion, 106th Cavalry Regiment, and the 776th Tank Destroyer Battalion broke through the German lines and blasted 30 miles through enemy territory. By late evening the Americans arrived at the doorstep of Bad Orb and liberated Stalag IX-B.

Stalag IX – B POW Camp, Bad Orb, c. 1945 (*U.S. Army Signal Corps*)

Chapter Seventeen

Seizing Bad Orb, April 1945

Once the Americans liberated Bad Orb, they focused on the health and welfare of the captives. They also seized all documents relating to the prisoners, gathered thousands of reports, letters, and pieces of paperwork, and handed them to translators, Red Cross officials, and the Military Intelligence Service.

Elements of the 2nd Infantry Battalion, 114th Infantry Regiment, 44th Division liberate 6,000 POWs, April 2, 1945 (*National Archives and Records Administration*)

Victor Akimoto's Soldier Individual Pay Record showed up within those records, detailing Victor's military career including immunizations, pay records, and references to his reduction in pay due to his voluntary demotion in rank.

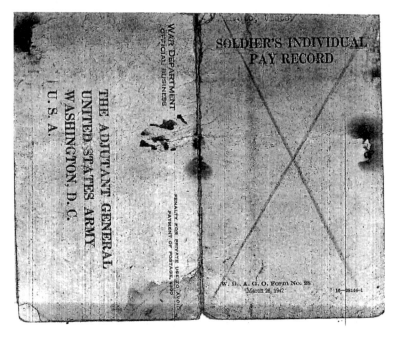

Victor Akimoto's Soldier Individual Pay Record. Victor's name appears in the top of the cover on the right hand side. (*U.S. Army*)

Several of the seized files pertained specifically to Victor and detailed the circumstances of his amputation. These files were subsequently classified by the U.S. Army and not shared with his family.

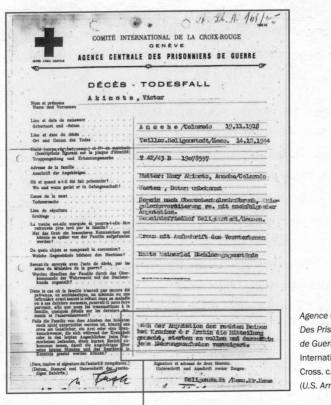

Agence Centrale Des Prisonniers de Guerre, International Red Cross. c. 1945 (U.S. Army)

German

Nach der Amputation des rechten Beines hat Kranker der Artzin die Mitteilung gemacht, sterben zu wollen und daraufhin jede Nahrungsaufnahme verweigert.

English Translation

Following the amputation of the right leg, the patient informed the doctor that he wants to die (sterben zu wollen) and therefore refused all food (Nahrungsaufnahme).

Victor Akimoto died on December 14, 1944 and was buried in the civilian cemetery in Seligenstadt, Germany, near the Reserve Lazarett Hanau military hospital. After the amputation of his leg, the doctors reported that Victor no longer wanted to live and he refused to eat.

According to the records, at 3 p.m. on December 22, 1944, a military procession with honor guard composed of other POWs convened and placed a wreath of pine boughs over Victor's grave. Next to his body in the snow-covered ground, a small glass bottle holding a slip of paper with his name and serial number was placed. No records confirm the use of a cross or other grave marker to identify his burial site. However, white crosses at Bad Orb and other German POW camps occasionally marked the graves of the dead. Six months passed from the time of Victor's capture to when his family received notification of his death.

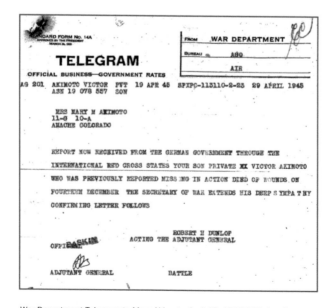

War Department Telegram to Mary Akimoto, April 19, 1945 (*U.S. Army*)

A few weeks after the liberation of Bad Orb, the War Department sent a telegram to the Akimoto family in Amache. Grave registration and mortuary officials within the U.S. Army had exhumed Victor's body from German soil, identified the remains with the help of the note in the glass bottle, and brought him back to France.

The War Department telegram of April 19, 1945 and the official letter dated May 8, 1945 (Victory in Europe Day) simply reported Victor's death. Communications with the Akimoto family did not mention Victor's capture, POW status, or his severe injury.

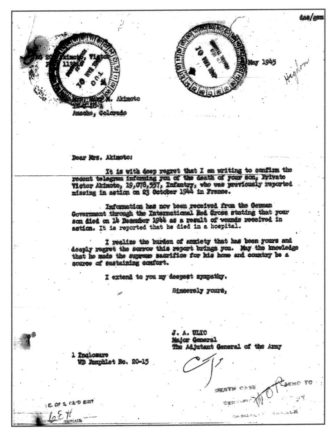

War Department letter to Mary Akimoto, May 8, 1945 (*U.S. Army*)

REQUEST FOR DISPOSITION OF REMAINS

GRADE OF DECEASED, NAME, ARMY SERIAL NUMBER AND REPORTED PLACE OF BURIAL

BUDGET BUREAU NO. 41-R217.

DATE:

Pfc John Akimoto, 37 344 336
Plot A, Row 12, Grave 142,
United States Military Cemetery
Vada, Italy

24 November 1947

| A | | C |
| B | | D |

DO NOT WRITE ABOVE THIS LINE

NOTE.—The next of kin should familiarize himself with the contents of the pamphlet, "Disposition of World War II Armed Forces Dead," before filling out this form. When the proper part of this form is filled out and properly signed by the next of kin, it should be returned to the OFFICE OF THE QUARTERMASTER GENERAL, MEMORIAL DIVISION, WAR DEPARTMENT, WASHINGTON 25, D. C., in the self-addressed postage-free envelope provided for this purpose.
If you are the next of kin or authorized representative of next of kin and desire to direct the disposition of the remains, please fill in PART I of this form.

PART I

MR & MRS.
I, Masanori Akimoto (_____)
(PLEASE PRINT OR TYPE THE NAME OF NEXT OF KIN) _____ (Please indicate relationship to the deceased by placing an "X" in the proper box.)

☐ WIDOW   ☐ WIDOWER   ☐ SON OVER 21 YEARS OLD   ☐ DAUGHTER OVER 21 YEARS OLD

☒ FATHER   ☒ MOTHER   ☐ BROTHER OVER 21 YEARS OLD   ☐ SISTER OVER 21 YEARS OLD

☐ RELATIONSHIP OTHER THAN ABOVE (Specify)

HAVING FAMILIARIZED MYSELF WITH THE OPTIONS WHICH HAVE BEEN MADE AVAILABLE TO ME WITH RESPECT TO THE FINAL RESTING PLACE OF THE DECEASED DESIGNATED ABOVE, NOW DO DECLARE THAT IT IS MY DESIRE THAT THE REMAINS: (Please place an "X" in the box opposite the option you have selected.)

☒ 1. BE INTERRED IN A PERMANENT AMERICAN MILITARY CEMETERY OVERSEAS. St Avold, France

☐ 2. BE RETURNED TO THE UNITED STATES OR ANY POSSESSION OR TERRITORY THEREOF FOR INTERMENT BY NEXT OF KIN IN A PRIVATE CEMETERY

(NAME AND LOCATION OF CEMETERY)

☐ 3. BE RETURNED TO _____ THE HOMELAND OF THE DECEASED OR NEXT OF KIN, FOR INTERMENT BY NEXT OF KIN IN A
(FOREIGN COUNTRY)

PRIVATE CEMETERY LOCATED AT _____
(LOCATION OF CEMETERY SELECTED)

☐ 4. BE RETURNED TO THE UNITED STATES FOR FINAL INTERMENT IN A NATIONAL CEMETERY LOCATED AT _____
(LOCATION OF NATIONAL CEMETERY SELECTED)

(Please indicate if your own religious services at a location other than the selected national cemetery are desired by "X" in the space below.) ☒ YES   ☐ NO

THE NAME OF THE DECEASED, THE SERIAL NUMBER AND GRADE ARE CORRECT EXCEPT FOR THE FOLLOWING CHANGES (Please make corrections and verify this fact by inserting the word "NONE" in the space below.)

None Side by Side Burial Overseas
Pvt Victor Akimoto 19078557
St Avold France III-2-19

DONG FORM 345 MILITARY

PAGE 1

Request for Disposition
of Remains Form in the
Individual Deceased
Personnel File for Johnny
Akimoto, November 24,
1947 (*U.S. Army*)

On May 8, 1945, the German high command officially surrendered, and the war in Europe ended. Allied troops around the world celebrated victory, while at the same time, the Soviet Union and America turned their full attention to defeating the Empire of Japan.

After the war, Mary and Masanori gave permission to the War Department to bury Victor with his fellow American soldiers in France. The family also requested that Johnny's remains be removed from Italy and placed next to Victor's, so they could rest together, in the beautiful, Lorraine American Cemetery near St. Avold, France. Johnny Akimoto lies in Plot A, Row 14, Grave 42. Next to him are the remains of his courageous brother, Victor Akimoto, in Plot A, Row 14, Grave 43.

— CHAPTER EIGHTEEN —

POSTWAR: WHAT BROTHERS DO

Ted Akimoto wondered for years why he was never ordered into battle. During World War II, he thought his stateside, noncombat assignments must had been related to the Sullivans, a group of five brothers who died after a Japanese submarine torpedoed their ship the U.S.S. *Juneau*, in November 1942.

Ted Akimoto, c. 1945 (Akimoto Family Collection)

There were also the four Niland brothers, two of whom died in rapid succession during the war. The U.S. Army managed to pull one from the battlefields of France, and the fourth brother survived the war in a Japanese POW camp in Burma. Moviegoers familiar with *Saving Private Ryan* know this story well. Ted Akimoto figured he remained out of combat because the U.S. Army did not want his parents to lose another son like the Sullivans and Nilands.

He did not learn the truth until years later. Through his military sources, he discovered the full impact of the meeting that had taken place in 1943 between Victor, the chaplain, and his company commander.

Ted Akimoto

If you are interested in learning more about Ted Akimoto, visit:
http://streams.wgbh.org/online/specials/war/akimoto/index.html

Ted Akimoto in General Douglas MacArthur's plane, *Bataan*, c. 1945 (Akimoto Family Collection)

As the oldest son, Victor believed it was his duty to look after his younger brothers. As any good son would do, he had promised his mother to keep Ted and Johnny safe. Yet the U.S. Army decided to keep sergeants of the 100th Infantry Battalion stateside to continue training new soldiers. In order for his commander to give him permission to go, Victor accepted a voluntary demotion from the rank of sergeant to private.

During that same conversation in 1943, Victor had also asked the chaplain and commander to make him a promise: to neither send Ted into battle nor allow Ted to take a reduction in rank to go into battle like Victor. Ted desperately wanted to join the 442nd Regimental Combat Team in combat, but his commander refused. Ted was offered two choices: become a paratrooper or enter Officer Candidate School. The 442nd Regimental Combat Team had no paratroopers associated with it. Thus Officer Candidate School became the only path open to Ted. He became a second lieutenant, known as a "90-day-wonder" because of the required three months of training. After four years of non-combat service, Ted received an honorary medical discharge from the Army after the removal of one of his kidneys.

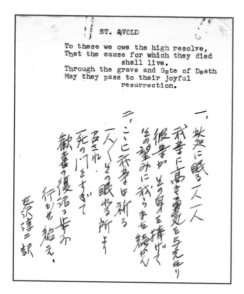

ST. AVOLD

To these we owe the high resolve,
That the cause for which they died
shall live.
Through the grave and Gate of Death
May they pass to their joyful
resurrection.

一、此処に眠人人

我等に高き覚悟を与え元

彼等が其の身を捧げて

死にゝその望みに我らまをも続べん

一人その眠る所より

此処に我等は祈る

死の門をすぎて

歓喜の復活の半か

行わも給え。

荒澤達二訳

Dedication from the Lorraine American Cemetery opening ceremony program. Japanese translation provided by Mary Akimoto, July 6, 1960. (Akimoto Family Collection)

Masanori, who died in 1951, never visited the graves of Victor and Johnny. However, 15 years after the war ended, on July 19, 1960, Ted and his mother Mary attended the dedication ceremony of Lorraine American Cemetery in France as guests of the U.S. Army.

A grand procession that day, including a number of military speakers and Mrs. Theodore Roosevelt, witnessed the dedication of the cemetery. When the ceremony was finished, Ted and Mary had a chance to visit the graves of Victor and Johnny and reflect on the tremendous sacrifices they had made.

In Flanders fields the poppies blow
Between the crosses row on row,
That mark our place; and in the sky
The larks, still bravely singing, fly
Scarce heard amid the guns below.

We are the Dead. Short days ago
we lived, felt dawn, saw sunset glow,
Loved and were loved, and now we lie,
    In Flanders fields.

Take up our quarrel with the foe:
To you from failing hands we throw
The torch; Be yours to hold it high.
If ye break faith with us who die
We shall not sleep, though poppies grow
    In Flanders fields.

John McCrae (1872-1918) Canadian
Medical Service

Flanders Field poem by John McCrae printed in the opening ceremony program at Lorraine American Cemetery, July 19, 1960. (Akimoto Family Collection)

Mary and Ted Akimoto standing between the graves of Victor and Johnny, July 19, 1960. (Akimoto Family Collection)

As Ted stood in the special section of the cemetery designed for 30 pairs of brothers, all killed in the war, he knew he too could have died and been buried in Plot A, Row 14, Grave 44. Victor had saved Ted's life with the bargain he struck with his commander and Ted would never forget this. Ted went on to live a full life, a grateful life. He felt he needed to live an honorable life not only for himself, but for Johnny and Victor as well.

After graduating from Arizona State University, he started a family and became a beloved art teacher at a Department of Defense

School, Munich American High School, in Germany. When Ted retired from a lifetime of giving to students, he took the time to write his memoirs. Ted Akimoto died in 2011. His memorial was attended by over 200 people, many of whom were former high school art and photography students.

Dotty K. Phipps

(One of Ted Akimoto's students at Munich American High School)

April 27, 2015

He was always smiling and so easy going, as a teacher, and that made him easy to talk to. He GLOWED when you "got it" or did really well on a project. I'll never forget this as long as I live: He was standing in front of my art class (86 or so) and talking about sculptures or something along that line when he asked, "Do you know why Michelangelo's Moses has horns?" and me, being a trivia buff and a big reader shot my hand up and said, "Oh, I know! Because the Hebrew word for horns and ray of light are the same." My goodness the look on his face – part shocked, part proud like I'd just won a spelling bee! I impressed him and he was not expecting it! He broke out into a thousand-watt grin, pointed at me and almost shouted, "Yes!!" I'll never forget that look, or the feeling of pride that welled up inside me, ever. His opinion meant the world to me. I wish I could've told him in person before he passed.

Ted Akimoto holding his photo of General MacArthur and Eisenhower (Akimoto Family Collection)

LORRAINE AMERICAN CEMETERY

2015

In the fall of 2014, the American Battle Monuments Commission established a partnership with National History Day and the Roy Rosenzweig Center for History and New Media at George Mason University to recruit teachers to tell the stories of fallen World War II soldiers. The goal: create lessons for students about the sacrifices of World War II in Northern Europe.

During the research process, Ted Akimoto's daughter, Sara, and his wife, Summer, contacted the author. Their guidance and support made an enormous difference in the course of this project. Later, the dedicated efforts of Lynne O'Hara at National History Day, historian Dr. Christopher Hamner at George Mason University, and an untold number of people at the National Records and Archives Administration and the U.S. Army provided piles of documents. With their support, declassified documents and military records for both Victor and Johnny were made available. Prior to this project, those records had not been reviewed since World War II.

Some of the most astounding papers in the collection, the POW records for Victor, were in German. Many of the details retold above were taken from those records.

On Tuesday, January 27, 2015, the author received a preliminary translation with devastating news. Because the records had been classified, the Akimoto family members were unaware of the details of Victor's death. Due to the circumstances involved with Victor's passing, Sara Akimoto was contacted by the author so she could inform the extended family.

January 28, 2015

Sara,

It's hard to believe after working on Victor and Johnny for these months that I learn something new. The information I have for you today is not easy to hear, but I feel like I should share with you pieces of the story even if they are hard to say and tell.

This morning, I received a preliminary summary of the POW documents about Victor. The records include prison camp records and doctor's records as well. There is no easy way to tell this to you, so I'm just going to tell you.

This is what the translator wrote to me this morning:

"This is the death certificate of an American soldier in 1945 who obviously was imprisoned in a German war prison camp. He was buried in Germany. He had a shot wound in the leg, then an infected sepsis and after amputation was done he informed his Doctor that he wanted to die and refused food intake."

The translator, a German, was very moved by the details and expressed those thoughts as well.

Bless you and your family,

Matt

The most disturbing detail to reveal to Sara—Victor's refusal to take food after the amputation—must have come as a shock. After everything he survived, in the end, Victor wanted to die.

Considering Victor's final days, a number of motives for his final decision could help explain his choice to stop eating. Perhaps he suffered from diarrhea as well, and the food would have made it worse. It is also possible that Victor refused to eat to allow other prisoners more food, as a gift. If this were the case, his father would have been proud that the family legacy of generosity prevailed. Or, perhaps Victor knew full well, after suffering from his injury for over seven weeks that he would not be able to recover. Soldiers like Victor, those who had experienced battle for long periods, would have known about sepsis. This type of infection, prior to antibiotics like penicillin, nearly always led to death under these conditions. An amputation was Victor's last hope to stop the infection.

Alternatively, Victor may not have wanted to return home as a broken soldier. From his perspective, perhaps life with a missing leg would have been too difficult, too dishonorable. He may have considered coming home suffering from a severe injury, an infection, and after spending time as a POW too humiliating. From all indications, Victor was a true warrior. Having to return home with a missing limb might have been more than he could accept.

By the next morning, Sara responded to the author's email.

January 29, 2015

Dear Matt,

You are very kind to worry about me and my family's feelings about this. I experienced a complex array of emotions, both after the initial reading and then upon reflection. I am grateful that our grandparents and presumably our parents (the remaining 6 siblings including my father) did not live long enough to learn this. I think if my dad had known the details he never would have revealed them to anyone. I know that all 3 brothers routinely lied about conditions and horrible atrocities in their letters to spare their parents, who were already interned in the camps. I also find myself incapable of judging Victor's decision with anything but love, sorrow and unnecessary forgiveness... no one can know the pain or awful conditions he may have endured before coming to that terrible decision. Perhaps the last one he felt he had any control over, if he truly believed he would never be rescued or see his family again....Maybe I would have come to the same decision.

Thank you for being so sensitive and careful in your wording. For better or for worse, the truth is the truth and I will always be grateful to you for caring deeply enough to find it.

Respectfully,

Sara

The first group of *Understanding Sacrifice* teacher scholars visit the graves of Victor and Johnny Akimoto at Lorraine American Cemetery in July 2015.

POSTSCRIPT: UNDERSTANDING SACRIFICE

World War II, by any measure, became the greatest calamity in human history caused by man. Overall, the world witnessed the destruction of over 60 million lives between 1939 and 1945. Estimates vary, but the Soviet Union may have lost over 25 million in defense of its homeland, while China may have lost an additional 50 million civilians. Germany suffered eight million deaths to a regime that cared little for its citizens. The wanton destruction of Hitler's Final Solution witnessed the murder of between six and twelve million Jews. The United States, whose contribution to the Allied victory can never be overlooked, lost more than 405,000 service members in the defense of freedom.

Awards and Honors

The 442nd Regimental Combat Team received over 18,000 individual decorations making them the most decorated unit in U.S. military history.

- 21 Medals of Honor
- 52 Distinguished Service Crosses
- 1 Distinguished Service Medal
- 559 Silver Stars
- 22 Legion of Merit

- 15 Soldiers' Medals
- 4,000 Bronze Stars
- 8 Presidential Unit Citations
- 1 Congressional Gold Medal
- 9,486 Purple Hearts

Given these numbers, it is hard to put into context the sacrifice of any one individual such as Victor or Johnny. Certainly they had "given it their all," in Ted's words. While 120,000 Japanese Americans encountered racism, bigotry, segregation, and incarceration, Japanese-American soldiers constituted over 33,000 members of the American military—including 6,000 soldiers in the Military Intelligence Service. Among the nearly 14,000 Japanese-Americans who served in combat units, nearly 10,000 earned Purple Heart Medals, including Victor Akimoto. The Japanese-American soldiers of this generation took up the battles of World War II with an esprit de corps that defies understanding.

Medal of Honor

More than 55 years later, 21 Asian-American veterans of the conflict, including 19 who served in the 100th Infantry Battalion and the 442nd Regimental Combat Team, had their Distinguished Service Crosses upgraded to Medals of Honor. This belated action aimed to remedy prejudice that existed at the time.

The Akimoto family and most other Japanese Americans faced tremendous animosity and hatred during and after World War II. At times in America, issues of race and religion come into conflict with patriotism. Incensed about the bombing of Pearl Harbor, the American public turned against Asians, in particular Japanese-Americans. In the same way some Americans sought revenge against Muslim-Americans for the 9/11 attacks, Japanese Americans became scapegoats for the sunken ships at the bottom of Pearl Harbor.

Veteran Terry Shima accepts the Congressional Gold Medal, presented by President Barack Obama, on behalf of Japanese American soldiers of World War II. (*Japanese American Veterans Association*)

Often the media, governments, and historians fail to acknowledge the savagery of war and celebrate instead the gallantry, glamour, and courage that wars occasion. According to military history professor

Congressional Gold Medal

On October 5, 2010, President Barrack Obama signed S.1055, a bill to grant the Congressional Gold Medal, collectively, to the 100th Infantry Battalion, 442nd Regimental Combat Team, and Military Intelligence Service, in recognition of their dedicated service during World War II.

Dr. Christopher Hamner of George Mason University, "War is always ugly. While World War II was certainly a necessary conflict against a thoroughly evil regime, defeating that regime required people and nations to engage in all sorts of cruel, vicious, and dehumanizing behaviors. It is tempting to omit the grisly details of the war–bodies burned by jellied gasoline, cities of civilians reduced to ashes and rubble, and countless families like Victor's suffering the permanent loss of a beloved father, son or brother–in favor of simply re-telling the courageous and inspiring story of the Rangers at Pointe-du-Hoc. But when we do that, we tacitly contribute to the glorification of the war–and at that point, we are not telling the whole truth."

Pointe-du-Hoc

During the landings at Normandy, France, the U.S. Army Ranger Assault Group commanded by Lieutenant Colonel James Earl Rudder assaulted and captured a pivotal point of land from the entrenched German Army. If you are interested in learning more, visit: **http://go.usa.gov/3AfV3**

Johnny's death brought home to the Akimoto family a very real truth. Victor, despite his best efforts as the older son, proved unable to protect his younger brother from one of the most common ancillary causes of death during war, infection.

As much as society wants to believe in the heroes and glory of war, not everyone in the military perishes from a single shot through the heart while undertaking a courageous deed. Soldiers die from bombs dropped by their own planes; soldiers die from tanks accidentally driving over infantrymen; and soldiers die from liver failure and infection. No matter the cause, a dead soldier never comes marching home.

Understanding Victor Akimoto's death requires thought, and considerable understanding. When the Germans "captured" Victor lying on his stretcher with a severe leg injury, they essentially signed his death certificate. They could have sent Victor and his medics back to the American lines. They decided not to. What then ensued, two months of suffering, brought Victor's life to an end. He must have held out hope that the sacrifices he had made for his brothers would someday be understood by his family. In fact, the sacrifices he made for Ted were entirely successful.

Ted lived a long and prosperous life, deeply indebted to the gifts of a brother he could never repay. Today, Americans can look upon Victor as a patriot and soldier of the highest order.

Standing between the crosses of 10,489 graves, Mary "Miki" Shiratori Akimoto keenly understood the devastating reality of war. To win World War II, many lives were sacrificed. True sacrifices, gifts willingly laid down "upon the altar of freedom," require acceptance, not repayment.[8]

The legacies of Johnny and Victor Akimoto, along with more than 405,000 American deaths of World War II, should be remembered, acknowledged, and honored.

About the American Battle Monuments Commission:

The American Battle Monuments Commission (ABMC) is a U.S. government agency charged with commemorating the service, achievements and sacrifice of the U.S. armed forces. Established by  Congress in 1923, ABMC administers, operates, and maintains 25 permanent American military cemeteries and 27 federal memorials, monuments and markers located across the globe. These cemeteries and memorials, most of which commemorate the service and sacrifice of Americans who served in World War I and World II, are among the most beautiful and meticulously maintained shrines in the world. For more information, visit **www.abmc.gov,** or connect with us on Facebook, YouTube, or Instagram.

About the Roy Rosenzweig Center for History and New Media

Since 1994, the Roy Rosenzweig Center for History and New Media (RRCHNM) at George Mason University has used digital  media to advance history education, preserve and present history online, and transform scholarship. RRCHNM is a democratic, collaborative space where scholars, developers, designers, and researchers work together to advance history education and digital humanities. For more information, visit **chnm.gmu.edu.**

About National History Day

National History Day (NHD) is a nonprofit education organization in College Park, Maryland. Established in 1974, NHD offers yearlong academic programs that engage over half a million middle and high school students around the 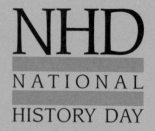 world annually in conducting original research on historical topics of interest. These research-based projects are entered into contests at the local and affiliate levels, where the top student projects have the opportunity to advance to the National Contest at the University of Maryland at College Park. NHD also seeks to improve the quality of history education by providing professional development opportunities and curriculum materials for educators. These take the form of webinars, professional development training, online courses for graduate credit, and summer institutes. NHD coordinates the Albert H. Small Normandy: Sacrifice for Freedom Student & Teacher Institute. For more information about NHD, visit **www.nhd.org**.

About ABMC's Education Initiatives:

ABMC launched its education initiative in 2013 with the intent to bring America's overseas cemeteries into American classrooms. These programs, created through partnerships with universities and non-profits, allow education experts to work with a small group of cross-disciplinary teachers to create and develop lesson plans and teaching ideas with a specific focus on ABMC's sites and resources.

Materials that are part of the ABMC education program are teacher-authored, standards-based, and reach across disciplines to introduce students to ABMC's resources and more importantly, the men and women we honor. This is in keeping with a promise made to families by General John J. Pershing, ABMC's first chairman, that "time will not dim the glory of their deeds."

ABMC's 2014–2015 program, which focused on World War II in northern Europe, has been managed by National History Day and the Roy Rosenzweig Center for History and New Media at George Mason University.

EPILOGUE

Mary "Miki" Shiratori Akimoto (1889 – 1979)

Mary lived a long life and enjoyed her 14 grandchildren. Her trip to France in 1960, for the opening of the Lorraine Cemetery in St. Avold, France, with her son Ted became one of her most cherished memories.

Masanori Akimoto (1876 – 1951)

Masanori survived the war years and got to meet some of his grandchildren including Steve, Marty, Jon, Carol, and Chris. He never visited the graves of his sons in France.

William "Bill" Kajikawa (1912 – 2010)

Bill left Arizona State University during World War II to join the 522nd Artillery Unit, part of the 442nd Regimental Combat Team. After leaving the Army he returned to ASU to be a football, basketball, and club baseball coach. As a coach, he was honored many times over for his contributions to the lives of young people. If you would like to learn more about Bill, visit:

https://asunews.asu.edu/20100215_Kajikawa_PassesAway

Jimmie Kanaya (1920 –)

A survivor of World War II's POW camps, Jimmie went on to a distinguished military career. He continues to speak, provide interviews, and lend his voice to documentaries to share his experiences of World War II.

If you are interested in learning more about the amazing life of Colonel Jimmie Kanaya, visit:
http://www.ww2online.org/view/jimmie-kanaya/segment-1 or
http://lcweb2.loc.gov/diglib/vhp/story/loc.natlib.afc2001001.21666/

Young Oak "Samurai" Kim (1919 – 2005)

Young Oak Kim remained in the military after World War II, achieving the rank of colonel. When he eventually settled down, he helped to start the Go for Broke Foundation in Los Angeles, which seeks to educate the public on the history of the 100th Infantry Battalion and the 442nd Regimental Combat Team. If you are interested in learning the extraordinary story of the first Korean American officer in charge of combat troops, visit:
http://www.goforbroke.org/oral_histories/oral_histories_video.php

Stanley Iwajigawa (1920 – 2014)

Stanley pulled Victor out of his foxhole and assisted him to safety. After World War II, Stanley took advantage of the GI Bill and attended college in Hawaii. After graduating in 1950, he became a teacher. He spent a lifetime educating children and working as a principal. He enjoyed windsurfing and hiking through the hills, valleys, and mountains of Hawaii. If you are interested in learning more about Stanley Iwajigawa, visit:
http://www.100thbattalion.org/archives/memoirs-and-journals/stan-izumigawa/

To: The Akimoto Family

We would like to take this opportunity to assure you that our family stands with you in honoring both of your fallen family heroes: Johnny and Victor Akimoto. Our father, Sergeant William Hardwick of the "The Lost Battalion," always wanted to find and thank the men of the 442nd RCT...for without their heroism and courage, he would not have returned to our family. His untimely death in 1972 prevented him from fulfilling his dream of finding and thanking the men who saved his life that bitter October in 1944. In his name, Susan and I, his daughters, have set about on a journey to find and thank those men and their families.

Simple words of "Thanks" seem inadequate in the face of such courage. Perhaps our best effort can be to make sure that you know that your loved ones will never be forgotten by our family – that we will speak their names in our homes and that their story will be told by generations that follow us. Victor and Johnny were honorable men and displayed great courage in the most challenging of circumstances.

In 2009, we traveled to the Vosges Mountains—the site of the rescue of the "Lost Battalion." There, in the deep woods, we stood with several of Victor's comrades and talked about that rescue. One of the veterans told us a story I would like to share with you.

"As we (the 442nd and Victor) walked up the trail into the woods to begin the rescue of your father, we were passed by troops coming back down the mountain. These troops yelled out to the 442nd saying, "Dont' go up there. You will die. Turn around." BUT, the men of the 442nd kept walking up the mountain."

I asked the veteran, "Why?"—"Why did you keep walking?"

He stood silently for a moment and finally said, "Because we were told we were their last hope."

That tells you all you need to know about Victor—that in the face of certain death, he kept walking—because his resolve was greater than self: the definition of a true hero.

So, their courage has provided a special bond for those of us left to tell their story—a golden thread of friendship and understanding—that from their sacrifices, we share a common spirit as we stand to remember and celebrate their contribution to our lives and to this country. They were, indeed, honorable men and true American patriots. We are blessed to be a part of their story.

Respectfully,

Janet Hardwick Brown
Susan Hardwick

Proud daughters of :   Sergeant William Hardwick
                        36th Division
                        141st Regiment
                        Company "B'
                        "The Lost Battalion"

Letter from the Hardwick family to the Akimoto family, September 25, 2015 (Akimoto Family Collection)

ENDNOTES

[1] It should be noted that Geisel later authored a number of children's books, including *The Sneetches* and *The Butter Battle Book*, that emphasized tolerance and working for peaceful solutions.

[2] Quoted in William Bruce Wheeler, Susan Becker, and Lorri Glover, *Discovering the American Past: A Look at Evidence, Volume II, Since 1985* (Boston: Wadsworth, 2012), 271.

[3] Seltex is a thin-coated paper product used to cover the outside or inside of walls to keep dust, dirt, and wind out of the internment camp barrack buildings.

[4] Nusus is a term borrowed from Japanese which means a disobedient person.

[5] Mail back to the states from soldiers was often delayed by weeks or even months. By the time this short postcard arrived, Johnny's parents had been informed via U.S. Army telegram that Johnny had died.

[6] William "Bill" Kajikawa was married to Margaret Akimoto, a sister of Johnny, Victor, and Ted. Bill was a member of the 522nd Field Artillery Battalion that eventually helped to liberate Holocaust survivors near Dachau.

[7] In 1962 the governor of Texas, John Connally, made the members of the 442nd Regimental Combat Team "Honorary Texans" for their role in the Battle of the Lost Battalion.

[8] Abraham Lincoln, Gettysburg Address, November 19, 1863.

BIBLIOGRAPHY

2nd Bn. 442nd Regimental Combat Team infantrymen hike up a muddy road in the Chambois Sector, France. Photograph. October 14, 1944. The U.S. Army Center of Military History (SC253983). http://www.history.army.mil/html/topics/apam/100-442_photos.html.

"7 Utahns Dead, 7 Wounded, 1 Safe, 1 Freed, 2 Lost." *The Salt Lake Tribune*, May 3, 1945: Sec 2, 6.

"442nd Organizational Chart." Sons and Daughters of the 442nd Regimental Combat Team. Accessed February 22, 2015. http://442sd.org/category/442nd-organizational-chart/.

442nd Regimental Combat Team, World War II Operations Reports, 1941-1948; Records of the Adjutant General's Office, 1917-, Record Group 407 (Box 17031); National Archives at College Park, College Park, MD.

442nd Regimental Combat Team, September 1944 - January 1945; World War II Operations Reports, 1941-1948, Records of the Adjutant General's Office, 1917-, Record Group 407 (Box 17034); National Archives at College Park, College Park, MD.

"Akimoto and Yasuda will report to Denver April 6." *Granada Pioneer*, March 31, 1943. http://cdmweb.lib.csufresno.edu/cdm/ref/collection/SVJAinWWII/id/1291.

Akimoto Family Photographs. 1890 - 2011. Courtesy of the Sara
   Akimoto.

Akimoto, Ted. *Various Photographs from Japan*. Photographs. 1945.
   World War II Road Show, University of Massachusetts at Boston.
   http://www.massmemories.net/WWII.php?pageNum_Images=2.

Akimoto, Ted. "Memoirs of Theodore Akimoto." Akimoto Family
   Collection. Boston, Massachusetts.

Akimoto, Theodore. *Collection of military photographs, various
   locations in postwar Japan*. Black and White Photographs. August
   1945 to February 1946. Akimoto Family Collection.

Akimoto, Theodore. "World War II Japan After the Surrender."
   Photograph narration. Audio File, 8:32. WGBH Educational
   Foundation. http://streams.wgbh.org/online/specials/war/
   akimoto/index.html.

Albers, Clem. *Arcadia, California. Evacuees of Japanese Ancestry
   from San Pedro, California, Arrive by Special Trains for Santa Anita
   Assembly Center...* Photograph. April 5, 1942. National Archives and
   Records Administration (537038). https://catalog.archives.gov/
   id/537038?q=santa%20anita%20arrive.

"Americans in German Prisoner of War Camps." Indiana Military Organization. Accessed February 22 2015. http://www.indianamilitary.org/German%20PW%20Camps/SoThinkMenu/GermanPW-START.htm.

"Anzio 1944." U.S. Army Center for Military History. Last modified January 21, 2010. Accessed February 22 2015. http://www.history.army.mil/brochures/anzio/72-19.htm.

Asahina, Robert. *Just Americans: How Japanese Americans Won a War at Home and Abroad.* New York: Gotham, 2006.

"Asian American and Pacific Islander Heritage Month: Honoring Japanese-Americans from the 442nd." American Battle Monuments Commission. Accessed February 22, 2015. http://www.abmc.gov/news-events/news/asian-american-and-pacific-islander-heritage-month-honoring-japanese-americans#.VOmqC7COHfa.

Brown, Raymond. *Prisoner of War Camp Stalag IX-B, Bad Orb, Germany.* Map. 1945. Indiana Military. http://www.indianamilitary.org/German%20PW%20Camps/Prisoner%20of%20War/PW%20Camps/Stalag%20IX-B%20Bad%20Orb/Pete%20House/Life/House-Pete-Life.pdf.

"Bruyeres and Biffontaine." Go for Broke National Education Foundation. Accessed February 22, 2015. http://www.goforbroke.org/history/history_historical_campaigns_bruyeres.php.

Chakales, L. S. "Nisei Japanese on Our Side Make Crack Regiment of the War." *San Antonio Express*, October 21, 1945: 6.

The Denver Post. "Amache Japanese-American Internment Camp." The Archive. Last modified February 26, 2013. Accessed February 22, 2015. http://blogs.denverpost.com/library/2013/02/26/amache-japanese-internment-camp/6790/.

Door of barber shop owned by Andy Hale, in a little desert town of Parker, 15 miles from where is located the Colorado River Relocation Center... Photograph. November 11, 1944. National Archives and Records Administration (210-CC-IN-4).

Dumas, Jerry. "He loved country, even when country didn't love him." *Greenwich Time*, February 2, 2011. http://www.greenwichtime.com/local/article/Dumas-He-loved-country-even-when-country-didn-t-992907.php.

Duss, Masayo. *Unlikely Liberators: The Men of the 100th and 442nd.* Honolulu: University of Hawaii, 1987.

"Executive Order No. 9066, February 19, 1942." National Archives and Records Administration. Accessed August 4, 2015. http://www.ourdocuments.gov/doc.php?flash=true&doc=74.

Flagg, J.M. *I Want YOU for the U.S. Army.* Broadside. 1917. The Library of Congress. http://www.loc.gov/exhibits/treasures/trm015.html.

Foster, Renita. "March to Freedom Filled with Danger." Japanese American Veterans Association. Modified October 2007. Accessed December 15, 2014. http://www.javadc.org/March%20to%20Freedom%20Filled%20with%20Danger%20by%20Renita%20Foster.htm.

Geisel, Theodore. *Waiting for the Signal from Home*. Political Cartoon. February 13, 1942. University of California, San Diego Library. http://library.ucsd.edu/speccoll/dswenttowar/index.html#ark:bb5222708w.

General of the Army Dwight D. Eisenhower. Portrait Photograph. November 18, 1947. Naval History and Heritage Command (USA P-16071). http://www.history.navy.mil/our-collections/photography/numerical-list-of-images/nara-series/USA-CC/USA-P-16071.html.

Grapes, Bryan J. *Japanese American Internment Camps*. San Diego: Greenhaven, 2001.

"Horace (Stanley) Kango Sagara." 100th Infantry Battalion Veterans. Accessed February 22, 2015. http://www.100thbattalion.org/archives/photos/n-s/horace-stanley-kango-sagara/.

Ikeda, Tom. "Sites." Densho. Last modified February 20, 2015. Accessed February 21, 2015. http://www.densho.org/sitesofshame/facilities.xml.

"Jap-Americans Rescue Men of Lost Battalion." *Nevada State Journal*, November 8, 1944: 4.

Japanese-American Internment. Evanston: Nextext – McDougal Littell, 2000.

Japanese Attack on Pearl Harbor, Hawaii. Photograph. December 7, 1941. The Franklin D. Roosevelt Presidential Library and Museum (197288). https://catalog.archives.gov/id/197288.

"John Akimoto." American Battle Monuments Commission. Accessed February 22, 2015. http://www.abmc.gov/search-abmc-burials-and-memorializations/detail/WWII_40583#.VOmiA7COHfZ.

Kanaya, Jimmie. E-mail Correspondence. January 22, 2015.

Kanaya, Jimmie. "Out on patrol and being captured near the Lost Battalion." National World War II Museum. Last modified 2013. Accessed February 22 2015. http://www.ww2online.org/view/jimmie-kanaya/segment-3/60151.

Lincoln, Abraham. Gettysburg Address. National Archives and Records Administration. Accessed August 7, 2015. http://www.ourdocuments.gov/doc.php?flash=true&doc=36&page=transcript.

Masuda, Minoru, Hana Masuda, and Dianne Bridgman. *Letters from the 442nd: The World War II Correspondence of a Japanese American Medic*. Seattle: University of Washington, 2008.

McIlwain, James. "Soldiers and the Camps." Brown University. Accessed December 14, 2014. http://charlotte.neuro.brown. edu/~jamesmcilwain/SOLDIERS%20AND%20THE%20CAMPS.pdf.

Japanese-American Internment. Evanston: Nextext – McDougal Littell, 2000.

John Akimoto, Official Military Personnel File, Department of the Army, RG 319, National Archives and Records Administration - St. Louis.

John Akimoto, Individual Deceased Personnel File, Department of the Army.

Letters from Johnny Akimoto to Akimoto Family Members, 1942 - 1944. Courtesy of Gay Sato.

Letters from Victor Akimoto to Akimoto Family Members, 1942 - 1944. Courtesy of Gay Sato.

Lillquist, Karl. *Imprisoned in the Desert: The Geography of World War II-Era, Japanese American Relocation Center in the Western United States*. Ellensburg: Central Washington University, 2007. http:// www.cwu.edu/geography/geography-japanese-american-relocation-centers

Masuda, Minoru, Hana Masuda, and Dianne Bridgman. *Letters from the 442nd: The World War II Correspondence of a Japanese American Medic*. Seattle: University of Washington, 2008.

McClellan, Joe. *Granada Relocation Center, Amache, Colorado. A tense moment in the Amache - Prowers County all-star baseball game held in the center Sunday, September 12, 1943, in connection with the Amache Agricultural Fair. Amache won 20-9.* Photograph. National Archives and Records Administration (537325). https://catalog.archives.gov/id/537325?q=amache%20baseball

McIlwain, James. "Soldiers and the Camps." Brown University. Accessed December 14, 2014. http://charlotte.neuro.brown.edu/~jamesmcilwain/SOLDIERS%20AND%20THE%20CAMPS.pdf.

Memorial Service For Japanese American Soldiers Who Died In World War II. Photograph. c. 1945. Japanese American Archival Collection Imagebase, Sacramento State University http://digital.lib.csus.edu/cdm/ref/collection/jaac/id/632.

"Occupational Records for Akimoto, Masanori." Japanese Immigrants to the United States, 1887-1924. Brigham Young University, Idaho. Accessed February 22, 2015. http://abish.byui.edu/specialCollections/fhc/Japan/occupations.asp?name_id=1806.

"Photo Gallery: Battalion Scrapbook." *The Honolulu Advertiser.* Last modified June 17, 2007. Accessed February 22, 2015. http://the.honoluluadvertiser.com/article/2007/Jun/17/ln/scrapbook.html.

This photograph depicts an American Liberty ship as it is loaded with supplies in Boston. Photograph. 1944. National Archives and Records Administration (7385015). Image. https://catalog.archives.gov/id/7385015?q=liberty%20ship

"Prisoners of War." 100th Infantry Battalion Veterans. Accessed February 22, 2015. http://www.100thbattalion.org/history/veterans/prisoners-of-war/.

Records for Victor Akimoto; World War II Army Enlistment Records, 1938-1946 [Electronic File], Record Group 64; National Archives at College Park, College Park, MD [retrieved from the Access to Archival Databases at http://aad.archives.gov/aad/fielded-search.jsp?dt=466, December 1, 2014].

Records for Victor Akimoto; World War II Prisoners of War Data File, 12/7/1941-11/19/1946 [Electronic File], Records of the Office of the Provost Marshal General, Record Group 389; National Archives at College Park, College Park, MD [retrieved from the Access to Archival Databases at http://aad.archives.gov/aad/fielded-search.jsp?dt=466, February 22, 2015].

"Rome-Arno Campaign." Go for Broke National Education Foundation. Accessed February 22, 2015. http://www.goforbroke.org/history/history_historical_campaigns_rome.php.

Ronald Reagan signing the Civil Liberties Act of 1988. Photograph. August 10, 1988. Ronald Reagan Presidential Library. http://www. reagan.utexas.edu/archives/photographs/large/c48754-4.jpg.

Roosevelt, Franklin D. *Americanism Is Not, and Never Was, a Matter of Race or Ancestry*. Washington, D.C. February 1, 1943. Speech.

Sara Akimoto to Matthew Elms Email Correspondence, 2015. Courtesy of Matthew Elms.

Second Lieutenant Jimmie Kanaya, Photograph. c. 1943. Courtesy of Jimmie Kanaya.

Soldiers of Company F, 2nd Battalion, 442nd Regimental Combat Team in the front lines near St. Die Area, France. Photograph. November 13, 1944. U.S. Army Signal Corps (SC341438). http:// www.history.army.mil/html/topics/apam/100-442_photos.html.

Steidl, Franz. *Lost Battalions: Going for Broke in the Vosges, Autumn 1944*. Novato: Presidio, 1997.

Summer Akimoto to Matthew Elms Email Correspondence, 2015. Courtesy of Matthew Elms.

Terry Shima: 2012 Presidential Citizens Medal Recipient. Photograph. March 11, 2013. White House. https://www.whitehouse.gov/ photos-and-video/video/2013/03/11/terry-shima-2012- presidential-citizens-medal-recipient.

"Through A Soldier's Eyes." November 7, 2014. PBS Video. http://video.tpt.org/video/2365361244/.

Teraoka, Moriso. *Soldiers Preparing For A 25-Mile Training Hike.* Photograph. March 1944. The Nisei Story: Americans of Japanese Ancestry During WWII, University of Hawaii. http://memory.hawaii.edu/object/io_1195876954171.html.

"To Wager Everything." Army Live. Last modified May 20, 2014. Accessed March 24, 2015. http://armylive.dodlive.mil/index.php/2014/05/to-wager-everything/.

Trinh, Jean. "When Santa Anita Racetrack Was A Japanese Internment Camp Assembly Center." LAist. Last modified December 8, 2014. Accessed February 22, 2015. http://laist.com/2014/12/08/when_santa_anita_racetrack_was_a_ja.php#photo-8.

Two color guards and color bearers of the Japanese-American 442nd Regimental Combat Team stand at attention while their citations are read. Photograph. November 12, 1944. U.S. Army Signal Corps (SC196716). http://www.history.army.mil/html/topics/apam/100-442_photos.html.

U. S. Army Signal Corps. "POW Camp (Stalag IXB) near Bad Orb with American and Allied prisoners." April 4, 1945. United States Holocaust Memorial Museum. http://collections.ushmm.org/search/catalog/fv5455.

Various Still Photographs; Records of the War Relocation Authority, Record Group 210. National Archives at College Park, College Park, MD.

"Victor Akimoto." American Battle Monuments Commission. Accessed February 22, 2015. http://www.abmc.gov/search-abmc-burials-and-memorializations/detail/WWII_40584#.VOmiTbCOHfZ.

Victor Akimoto, Official Military Personnel File, Department of the Army, RG 319, National Archives and Records Administration - St. Louis.

Weintraub, T/5 Louis. *On April 2nd a task force of infantry and cavalry raided...* Photograph. April 2, 1945. U.S. Army Signal Corps (111-SC-339369). http://www.lonesentry.com/badorb/stalag_ixb_bad_orb_germany_photo_6.html.

Weintraub, T/5 Louis. *Here liberated Americans sitting outside their barracks, eat their first meal of "C" rations since December 15th.* Photograph. April 2, 1945. U.S. Army Signal Corps. http://www.lonesentry.com/badorb/.

Weintraub, T/5 Louis. *A task force of infantry and cavalry raided enemy held territory to release 6,000 Allied soldiers, 3,364 of which were Americans, from prison camp Stalag IX-B, Bad-Orb, Germany...* Photograph. April 2, 1945. U.S. Army Signal Corps. http://www.lonesentry.com/badorb/.

World War I Civilian Draft Registration, Bonneville County, Idaho -
1917-1918. US GenWeb Archives. Accessed February 22, 2015.
http://files.usgwarchives.net/id/bonneville/military/ww1/wwibnvA.
txt.

World War II Operations Reports, 1941-1948; Records of the Adjutant
General's Office, 1917-, Record Group 407 (Box 17049); National
Archives at College Park, College Park, MD.

*Young Oak Kim receives an award. Second Lieutenant Jimmie
Kanaya*, Photograph. c. 1944. The University of Southern California
Libraries. http://digitallibrary.usc.edu/cdm/compoundobject/
collection/p15799coll126/id/17845/rec/3.

INDEX

About the Author: Matthew Elms

When the Akimotos Went to War is Matthew's first published book. He wrote the book to highlight the true story of one Japanese-American family for young adult readers. The Akimoto tale brings together stories of the 100th Infantry Battalion, 442nd Regimental Combat Team, Japanese internment policies, and World War II.

Matthew, a social studies teacher at Singapore American School, lives with his wife, Dr. Deborah Elms, daughters Callie and Alicia, and son Cameron. He enjoys traveling around the world and sketching various people, places, things while waiting for dinner in restaurants. For extra fun, he enjoys making the lives of his eighth grade students difficult.